From Rags To Riches:
Success in Apparel Retailing

THE WILEY SMALL BUSINESS SERIES

For the small business owner, success or failure often depends on the day-to-day management of hundreds of business problems and details. Drawing on the knowledge and experience of experts, these concise, detailed handbooks offer you sound advice and vital practical help on every aspect of managing a small business—sales, financing, accounting, advertising, security, and taxes—everything you need to operate a successful business.

OTHER TITLES IN THE SERIES

Look for them in your favorite bookstore.

From Rags To Riches:
Success in Apparel Retailing

Marvin E. Segal
Executive Director,
Southwest Apparel
Manufacturers Association

1807 1982

JOHN WILEY & SONS, INC. NEW YORK CHICHESTER BRISBANE TORONTO SINGAPORE

Library of Congress Cataloging in Publication Data:

Segal, Marvin E.,
　From Rags to Riches: Success in Apparel Retailing.

(Wiley Small Business Series)

81-70848

ISBN: 0-471-09156-1

Printed in the United States of America

82,83　　10 9 8 7 6 5 4 3 2 1

*To my wife, Pearl; daughters Helene, Robin,
Debra; and son, Scott—who were inspirational.
And to the thousands of customers—
who were instructional.*

Contents

Preface

In my 25 years as a store manager, buyer, merchandise manager, and finally as the President and owner/partner of ladies' and men's specialty stores, I learned many things—but above all I learned that owning and managing your own retail store is a grueling challenge and one of the most rewarding experiences in life.

It has been said that nothing in this world worth having is gained easily. You will find out just how true this statement is when if you realize your ambition of having your own store.

If I may take the privilege of using my own experiences to point out the pitfalls and glories of owning your own retail store, it is merely to give you the benefit of what I have learned the hard way. And why shouldn't you take advantage—we do not *both* have to suffer the same mistakes!

After 20 years I sold my business (except for one store, since all merchants keep one in their back pocket) and accepted a position as Executive Director of an apparel association. This has been a unique experience and could be the material for another book.

I relate this little history for no other reason than to establish my credentials for what will follow. At various times in my career people would come to me for advice on opening a store. We would talk, and they would take notes and ask a thousand questions. After they left, I would recall the many other things I should have told them and would sit down and write them long letters. Over the years these long letters have developed into this book. Obviously no book, no matter how long, or any course on merchandising can replace experience. All I can hope to accomplish in the following pages is to prepare you to observe and listen with an eye and ear primed with general information.

So you want to open an apparel store! Why? If you think it's an easy way to *make a dollar,* or if you are tired of doing nothing and think that this would be a fun way of doing *something,* you are (as my daughter says) "wrong-o-wrong"!

Yet the retail business is one of the most rewarding experiences in the world: the thrill of watching what you have bought sell to a customer; the delight in having someone stop in front of a cleverly trimmed window, smile, and then come into the store and ask for the item; the excitement that comes with seeing your store's ad in the newspaper; the joy and satisfaction of driving up to your store and knowing that it is YOURS; the pride that comes with success. If these are your reasons for wanting to become a merchant, then welcome to the club. We have all been bitten by this bug. William Shakespeare in Act 4 of *Antony and Cleopatra* says; "to business that we love, we rise betimes and go to it with delight!"

The key word in the bard's wisdom is *love.* So many people are working at jobs that they not only do not love, but—worse still—do not even like. This can take the joy out of life. If when you get up in the morning you have to push yourself out of bed and force yourself to go to work because you dread the next eight hours, then you are working at something you should not, and a change is in order. Life is too short to make the majority of your waking hours sheer drudgery. Not everyone is meant to own his business or be his own boss. Some were meant to have a good steady job with all the side benefits that come from working for a successful firm. This is not to say that one is right and the other wrong; it merely shows that the world is made up of different people. If you fall into the category of those who want to be their own masters, then owning a store may be your answer.

With all this in mind let us progress to the art, or science, of management and what it will take for you to be a successful merchant.

Marvin E. Segal

Dallas, Texas, 1981

One

Management:
An Art Or A Science?

*Rembrandt and Einstein
never had to take markdowns.*

There is no start like a beginning. And there is no beginning without a definition of terms so that we shall be talking about the same thing.

What Is Management?

Management is that unique element without which you have no business. In the operation of a store it is easy to be lulled into a sense of false security by knowing that you are buying the right goods from the right resources, that you have competent (if not good) salespeople, that your windows reflect the image you wish to project, that your housekeeping is in order, that your location is good, and that you show up for work every day.

Notwithstanding all the above, if you do not have the element known as *management*, you will fail. The days of succeeding in spite of yourself are gone. And in today's competitive world, the good manager not only survives, but prospers.

1

To keep up with the competition, managers must manage! You must manage your *entire* business and not just *parts* of it, such as advertising or windows or sales. Managing means planning to avert problems before they become problems.

So what is a manager?

To answer this relatively complicated question I went to Mr. Webster, who had this to say:

> 1. *Act or art of management, conduct, control.* 2. *Judicious use of means to accomplish an end with skillfull treatment.* 3. *Capacity for managing, controlling, directing, caring for, guiding to achieve one's purposes.*

Now you know what Webster thinks of management; but how does this relate to you and the small store you wish to open?

The key word omitted from the above definition is WORK. Being a good manager requires unselfish dedication to the job. It means a constant updating of your knowledge with reference to your industry. It means total devotion to the task at hand. It means foregoing the salary you *could* now receive for the hope of the still greater money to be realized from owning a profitable business.

Management means allocating your time and capital to obtain maximum return from both. It means directing your every effort toward a realistic goal. It means being in love with what you're doing. It means control of your own destiny.

If you have been nodding *yes* as you read along, you are ready to read on—even if you are not ready to seek a location and sign a lease. But you *have* reached the place to start making decisions as to type of store, location, size, and capital investment, and to help you do all this is the purpose of this book.

However, to answer the question "What is management?" We really ought to get clear in our minds the simple answer to

---

* *Webster's Collegiate Dictionary,* fifth edition.

a more fundamental question: What is the purpose of a retail store? Only one: to earn a livelihood or profit for the operator of the business—YOU! Any other reason or explanation is secondary. All advertising, display, selling arts, buying—even your ability in the handling of customers and services you perform for them—are all calculated to produce basically one thing: A PROFIT. This is not mercenary, it is a fact of retail life!

Since we have now determined what a manager is and the purpose of a retail store, and since there are a hundred places to start and a thousand paths to follow, let us begin with the fundamentals.

Management is the art of getting things done through the proper use of people. Your duty as the manager of your business is to organize the work (yours and your employees'), delegate responsibility, motivate those under you, and to plan. Many research studies have been done on the subject of management and its importance to the successful operation of a business. The consensus of these studies seems to be that a deficiency of management training, or a lack of experience, or insufficient time devoted to all the various facets of management results in some 90 percent of all small-business failures.

Organizing Work

Organizing your work should eventually come as second nature. It is important that you relegate the various things that must be done in order of importance to make sure that *first things come first.* If this sounds elementary, that's because it is. It is fundamental. Yet this is the one area of management that is least heeded and most often overlooked. Unpacking a shipment comes *after* waiting on a customer but comes *before* changing a light bulb. Each of these functions is important in its own right, but it occupies a different rung on the ladder of importance, and each must be completed in its *own* proper time. It will be your responsibility as manager to determine what should come where on the scale of *things-I-must-get-done*. In a small operation this duty usually belongs to the boss.

If your people have too much idle time—that is, nothing to do—it usually means you have too much help. On the other hand, if your people have no free time, it can mean one of two things: (1) you may be a little short of personnel, or (2) you could be driving your help too hard. Either way, you must achieve a balance between the number of people working and the jobs that must be completed.

Delegation and Motivation

Do not be afraid to delegate responsibility. Final decisions always remain with the boss, but the actual carrying out of these tasks should be assigned to *competent* help as much as possible, leaving you to do the things that only you can do.

It is easy to fall into the traps of "If you want it done right, you have to do it yourself," or "It's easier to do it myself than explain what I want done," or "I can do it faster than I can explain it." One or all of the above may be true, but fight the temptation. Delegation of responsibility is more than a matter of making your life easier; it is an essential ingredient of a smooth operation and happy employee relationship. And a prime ingredient of successful delegation is motivation of your employees.

Motivation of those under you can be accomplished in a number of ways. First, of course, there is money. This is particularly true of sales help (which we will cover more fully in Chapter 11). *First* does not mean *most important* or the *only* way. Over the years, I have seen some very highly paid executives who were not motivated and who operated on less than full power. Remember, for the most part, people do not feel they are ever paid enough or fully appreciated.

Motivation can come by what you say and do as well as how much you pay. Compliments when a person is right, and constructive criticism when that person is wrong, can go a long way toward keeping your people on a well-motivated track.

Planning

In your role as a planner you are filling one of the most vital aspects of your operation. This is one duty that it is virtually impossible to delegate. To quote an old saying, "Plan your work and work your plan." It may be an old saying, but, like wine, it gets better as it gets older. No business, no matter how large or small, can operate without a plan.

When speaking of planning, we are not speaking of one all-inclusive way of projecting our final target area. There is a definite line between managing your business by the use of a plan that meets daily problems with a preconceived set of rules and planning with a definite objective in mind to be accomplished at a later date.

A preconceived set of *rules* puts the emphasis first on what actions are reasonable and workable and how they are to be carried out. Contrasted to this is the *objective*, which looks to a goal and then figures out how to achieve that goal.

Each of these two schools of thought has merit. Personally, I feel that using the "daily plan" first to obtain the "final goal" second is having the best of both worlds. Odd as it may sound, it makes business sense.

What all this boils down to is the art of long- and short-range planning. Management of a business can be likened to a chain running from anticipation to fulfillment, with planning being but one link. As with any chain, it is only as strong as its weakest link. The only difference here is, if planning is your weak link, it will weaken a sufficient number of other links to make the entire chain unusable.

Management: Legal Structure

Here it may not be out of place to discuss the three legal structures under which a business can be established: (1) a single (or sole) proprietorship, (2) a partnership, (3) a corporation. There are other ways (i.e., syndicates, joint stock companies), but these are not usually applicable to a small operation.

Single or Sole Proprietorship

The key words here are *single* or *sole*. You are on your own: you alone are the owner; you are the one responsible; and you have no one with whom to share the blame. This is the simplest way of going into business. For the small company, it can be the most flexible system of operation.

The toughest boss you will ever have will be you yourself. No one, not even your present employer (whom you think is tough), can ever be as hard on you as you yourself.

It has been said, "I used to work eight hours a day and had no worries; now I'm the boss, work 16 hours a day, and have all the worries."

In this type of operation the reliance on self-interest is the most outstanding motivation. This has been called being a "self-starter." For an employee, the rewards for this motivation can be higher wages, commissions, or rising up the corporate ladder. For the sole proprietor, it can mean profits.

As the individual owner, you and your business are as one. This total association of your name with your store will create a desire to do more than merely make money. You will strive for the respect of your customers and employees. This concern for your place in the community will govern much of your business practices. Drawback: in some cases the owner can be *personally* responsible for debts and taxes owed by the company.

Partnership

This is the easiest way for two or more people to go into business together. And in ease of operation, it has many of the same advantages as the single proprietorship. In addition, it has the advantage of sharing the responsibilities.

The most common name applied to a partnership is "firm." Most firms conduct business in the name of the firm rather than the names of the individual partners. The firm itself assumes a certain legal identity: it can receive and expend monies; it can be sued; it has its own name; and for the most part, it can conduct the affairs of the business. The partners can draw a salary and in certain cases can be sued as individuals.

There are different types of partnership: A *"General"* partnership can be involved in more than one type of business as opposed to a *"Particular"* partnership, which operates a single business.

In many partnerships, the individual partners can be held solely responsible for the debts of the entire business. For this reason some states permit a *"Limited"* partnership. Under this arrangement you, as a partner, have your liabilities limited to the actual amount invested. A limited partnership is akin to a corporation but does not sell stock to the general public.

Partners have defined responsibilities to the firm and to one another:

1. Each partner has the right to make all other partners adhere to the partnership agreement.
2. Each partner is responsible for the actions of his or her partners in the running of the business.
3. Each partner cannot use company money for personal debts and obligations.
4. Each partner may audit the firm's books at any time, and the exercise of this right cannot be prevented by any other partner.

Just as there are different types of partnerships, there are different types of partners, with each serving the company in

his or her own way. Partners fall into four major categories:
(1) *Active:* assumes the duties of managment; shares in the
profits and is liable for the losses. (2) *Secret:* is part of the firm
but is not known to the general public. (3) *Silent:* is not
involved in management but shares in profits and losses.
(4) *Nominal:* is involved in the day-to-day operations of the
business but does not share in the profits.

Drawback: if you and your partner(s) are not kindred
souls, the whole situation could become a very unhappy
experience.

Corporation

This is the most structured way to form a business. A corporation is governed by state law and is a legal entity. It has a
sphere of activity and an identity all its own, spelled out by
charter. As an owner, you will be happy to know that corpor-
ations are taxed separately from executive salaries, with only
the corporation responsible for its taxes and debts, not you.

Again, a corporation is a legal entity created by law. In
reality the law has (in its Frankenstein power) created a person who can hold property, make contracts, file suits, and
conduct business. It is subject to laws that levy the same penalties as those imposed on a person. It can be sued, fined, and
even eliminated, but it cannot be sent to jail.

A corporation is usually formed by a coalition of three or
more people by applying for and receiving a state charter. In
the United States and Canada, the amount of property held
by a corporation is limited by law or charter. Most states levy
a corporation tax. This can be a fixed rate on the capital stock
or on the earnings of the corporation.

There are certain rules that apply when playing the corporation game:

    1. The corporation is organized by the stockholders.
    2. The corporation elects officers and the board of directors.

3. The corporation is responsible for the daily operation of the business.
4. The corporation sets salaries for the officers.
5. The corporation sets duties for the officers.
6. The corporate stockholders usually have as many votes as shares of stock they own.
7. Anyone owning 51 percent of the stock of the corporation can choose the officers and control policy.
8. The corporation may owe money but stockholders are not individually responsible. This does not apply if a stockholder has personally signed for a debt as an individual.

In determining which form you wish your business to take, you of course must take many factors into consideration, not the least of which is taxes. The final determination should really have the benefit of the expert advice of your accountant and attorney. Weigh all of the above factors and make your decision in concert with your advisors.

Two

Anatomy of a Merchant

In the body business...
the Merchant is the Heart.

Expertise

To put it more simply: *what do I know*? What do I know enough about on which to risk my money and time?

Only you can answer these questions. However, there are obvious avenues to explore. If you have a college degree, you must have studied *something* (how's that for an assumption?); but since there are no stores selling sociology or psychology, we can discount certain majors. Secondly, if you have been working at something, and if you are still working, you *must* have learned the rudiments of your job; therefore this would be as good a place as any to start.

Since my expertise is in the apparel industry I will, throughout this book, refer to this type of operation. You must remember, however, that *basic* business practices are basic business practices whether you are selling dresses or stationery.

Let us assume that since you wear clothes, or worked in a clothing store, or studied textiles in college, or just think you have a feeling for this business, you will open a small ready-to-wear specialty store. You have now taken the first step, deciding what your business will be. You have decided that your expertise (sometimes called *chutzpah*) lies in this direction.

Let us again assume for the moment that you think you can be an apparel merchant because you dress fairly well, like clothes, and believe you have a feeling for apparel. This assumption has led more would-be merchants down the primrose path than personality, good looks and a diploma. These attributes are not tantamount to executive ability, advancement, or the title of *merchant*.

The word *expertise* denotes *knowing something*. If you enter business with a knowledge of just how little you know, you are ahead of the game. The saying of Horace applies here: "Consider well what your strength is equal to, and what exceeds your ability." Never try to impress someone in any industry that you know more than you do, because after talking with you for five minutes, they will know exactly how much or little you really know.

So okay, you may not be an expert, but you want to become a merchant. What, then, is a merchant?

A Merchant Is. . .

A *merchant* is a "person whose business is buying and selling goods for a profit," according to Webster. This definition does not begin to tell the story of the years of experience, the long hours of hard work, and the knowledge required to *earn* the title of merchant.

We in America have become a nation of "shopkeepers" (as opposed to merchants) and "clerks" (as opposed to salespeople). Anyone can be a "shopkeeper," since the requirements are simple: carry a key, show up on time, and lock up at night. A "clerk" has only to write up the sale (which the customer has usually selected with no help or assistance) and put the purchase in a bag. A clerk does not even have to receive the money, because the cashier handles this task in most transactions.

A trade can be learned in many ways: apprenticeship, college, or through the school of experience (sometimes called on-the-job training), and yet no one can be *taught* to be a merchant. It takes an inborn feeling for sifting, time, a sixth sense of your customers' needs and desires, and your ability to understand and work within your industry.

If we are fully to comprehend the honored title of merchant (and I do not use this term any more lightly than the word *gentleman*, as there is not an overabundance of either), we must analyze the above ingredients.

Sifting

Sifting has been used by prospectors for centuries. Just as the Forty-niners of the last century panned for gold by sifting the river bottom sand, you as a merchant must sift through a maze of problems and experiences to find the gold that comes with a successful store. All buyers are exposed to a multitude of lines and pressure. The process of shopping and not succumbing to pressure can be called *sifting*. Always looking for that something new can be laborious and tedious, but it is an absolute necessity. To resist the razzle-dazzle and find the best dollar value for the dollar spent is the art of *sifting*.

This sifting process can be applied to salespeople, hiring of help, buying of services and supplies, plus the decision-making that you will be involved in every day. It is an ongoing effort and should become a way of life.

Consider the various options open to the merchant as so many grains of sand, and that hidden somewhere within this sand are the right ways of doing business. By sifting out the many erroneous factors, you will be left with only the elements conducive to a healthy operation.

As in all sifting processes, you may not be able to eliminate every distraction, every piece of misinformation, or every bad habit, but hopefully you will be able to refine your operation into a smoothly functioning business.

Timing:

We in the apparel business know the value and importance of having the right goods in the right place *at the right time.* Perhaps this industry, more than any other, lives or dies by *timing.* The selling time of a dress is limited and therefore must be in stock when your customer is ready to buy. Large stores, through their huge open-to-buys (discussed in Chapter 8), enjoy the privilege of being experimental. Small stores must follow suit at the right time. *Timing does not mean being first, it means not being too late.* If you fall too far behind, it can mean lost sales and big markdowns. When speaking of following the large stores' lead, I am referring merely to drastic changes in fashion (i.e., skirts up or down in length, leisure suits, etc.).

A perfect example of this happened in the 1950s. A dress style called the *chemise* became the talk of the industry. Large stores put as much as 60 percent of their dress stock and 100 percent of their advertising in this one style, which turned out to be the biggest bomb ever to hit the stores. Large stores weathered this storm and small shops were killed. The style lasted only a matter of a few months and then had to be marked down. I remember taking chemise dresses that cost (wholesale) $29.75 and selling them for $5.99 just to get them out of stock. Sometimes it's not a sin to be a follower.

True as this is, it is truer still in smaller stores. Large stores, with their chain of command, rarely afford their buyers the opportunity of talking with, or waiting on, the customers.

Their knowledge is derived largely from the stacks of reports they must read and prepare. Small stores, in addition, see the same customers over and over again. A certain rapport is built between the customer and the salesperson (if the salesperson is worth his or her salt). Proper lines of communication between you and that customer (or salesperson) can make you aware of what your customers need.

To Understand and Work Within Your Industry

This comes with experience. The mere exercise of opening your front door, going to market, and writing orders does not constitute either understanding or working within your industry. Understanding is knowing the nature of your trade as it relates to the manufacturer, to you as the merchant, and ultimately to the consumer—and applying it all to the running of your business.

Sixth Sense

A "sixth sense" in business does not require a crystal ball or tarot cards. There is no magic in business. Applying the proper amounts of education, dedication, and determination with equal amounts of proper business principles and practices constitutes this sense of being a merchant.

If there is such a thing as magic, it should be renamed "inspiration." A truly good merchant is inspired. This, combined with the five attributes listed above, form six business senses. And all of these factors taken together make for a "sixth sense."

A sixth sense can be acquired and learned from your customers. A real merchant talks to, and learns from, his or her own customers and develops this sense to know and thereby anticipate their needs. The knowledge gained on the floor of your store, combined with the messages brought to you by sales reps and manufacturers, gives you this feeling of knowing what's going to be right.

This is not to be confused with having to know everything about the manufacturing process. In fact, you do not even *want* to know too much about how a manufacturer figures cost. What you must know is if it will sell (in your store) at the price you must get for it at retail. I made it a point in my years as a buyer never to tell a manufacturer or their salesperson that they should make their garment cheaper. If I felt a garment was overpriced or would not bring the retail price demanded, I would simply pass that style by.

My grandfather was a small-town merchant in Minnesota. His inventory control system was simple. When he had emptied a box of shirts, he bought another box. Computers had not been invented and accountants had a simple method for figuring profit: take in the money, pay the bills, and what is left over is your profit. Inventory was not a factor in their thinking. They operated strictly by cliché #2: "You can't do business from an empty wagon." Using this philosophy, he was successful in his world of the Gay Nineties.

My father, a buyer and merchandiser for large stores during the 30s and 40s and a small store operator in the 50s, learned the importance of keeping tabs on inventory. In the 30s, economic conditions made it imperative not to be *overbought*, since paying bills was the number one problem facing merchants. In the 40s, because of the war, inventory control was a different problem. Owing to little civilian production, the wagon could become somewhat bare if you did not have friends among manufacturers who would include you in their allotments. The 50s brought postwar prosperity and recession. Both caused merchants to be on their toes or else.

I opened my first store in 1950. I first learned my trade in business courses in college. I was not the first to attend college, since both my father and grandfather were college-educated, but I was the first to study business. However, my education did not really begin until I entered the world of small business on my own, and the control of my inventory was one of my first lessons. I had it somewhat easier, since I entered this world attuned to computers.

I have given this family history for reasons other than family pride: our world of business has changed; we live in a much more complicated merchandising time than my grandfather and a much faster-paced time than my father. You will be entering a period even more advanced in merchandising techniques.

As we in the industry are quite aware, our business can be confusing enough without having to learn an entirely different operation. Even though the manufacturing sector is closely tied to the retail store, it is completely divorced from markup, cost of operation, purchasing, etc.

Never try to figure a manufacturer's cost. There are so many variables that go into the wholesale price that it becomes an impossible task for anyone not deeply involved in the process.

When you are accomplished in all I have spoken of—plus courtesy, hospitality, friendliness, and a love of what you are doing—then you are on your way to becoming a merchant and to practicing the art of creative management.

Three

Selecting a Location

*Life can be so sweet
on the busy side of the street.*

It has been said that a good salesperson could sell "iceboxes to Eskimos." What they did not tell you was he would have sold more if he had a better location!

A childrenswear shop next to a singles bar is hardly a good location. However, a record store next to a high school should do well. When you open your front door, it should be in the right area or on the right side of the street for the product you wish to sell.

Will It Be—Must It Be a Mall?

Today, America is a land of giant shopping malls. These super selling centers are usually anchored by two to four major stores and anywhere from 75 to 150 smaller stores in between, linked together by a covered mall. It is easy to be lulled into thinking that every customer in town flocks to these centers and that if *you* are not in with them you perish or, at least, have little chance for success. This is far from the truth! There are many successful small stores located in "open" and "strip" centers.

The merits and problems of these centers are discussed later. Simply defined, an *open* center is just what it says: a center not covered by a common roof, usually on four corners of a good intersection. A *strip* center is a group of small stores on one or both sides of a busy street. The strip center can be anywhere from one to several blocks in length and usually consists of smaller merchants without a *major* store to act as an anchor.

Your capital will determine the size and type of center you choose. To see the differences, let us examine each of these various centers individually, with its pros and cons.

The Regional Covered Malls

If it is a successful mall, space will be at a premium. This reverts to the basic economic formula of supply and demand. If you can get space in a successful mall, it will cost considerably more per square foot than other locations. For a small store just opening in a very competitive atmosphere and based on expected volume, the rent could be devastating. If operating capital is *not* a major problem, this may be the route to take.

Large centers usually do not assist (or else assist in a very small way) in the actual construction costs of putting in the store. Most covered malls will give you three unfinished walls and a concrete slab floor. The expense of getting the store ready to do business (i.e., installation of carpet or tile, ceiling, lights, air conditioning, glass front, fixtures, etc.) will vary from city to city *but are the expense of the tenant*.

Even though the expense of completing your store belongs to you, this is not to say you can not expect some assistance from the landlord. Some centers will give a *per square foot* allowance to help meet this expense.

At one of the last stores I opened, the center allowed us two dollars per square foot for this purpose. Since the store we were opening was 5000 square feet, our allowance amounted to $10,000. This was like a drop in the ocean when compared to the actual cost of completion, but it certainly helped. As one of the medium-sized tenants in the center, I was able to bring some additional pressure to bear. I insisted that I be paid as I presented paid bills to the landlord. As I finished a portion of the construction, I presented the bill to the land-lord. He in turn gave me the amount due the subcontractors and I paid them with the advance received from the landlord. In this way I postponed borrowing as long as possible and in so doing saved interest charges. I did not ask for anything unreasonable. And I did not expect to receive what a major store could expect to receive, so I was not disappointed.

The most important advantage of opening in a regional center is the traffic generated by the combined advertising of a large number of stores, plus the major stores' drawing-power in the center.

Small stores are by nature parasitic. That is to say, they live off the traffic created by the large stores. However, the competition in regional centers is fierce and it truly becomes a case of the survival of the fittest. This is not to say that a mer-chant who gives the customers what they want, when they want it, and at a price they expect to pay cannot, or would not, be successful.

Open and Strip Centers

Here we have almost the reverse of the factors that affect taking space in a regional mall. In a regional mall you have walking traffic, open and strip centers have driving traffic; the stores in regional malls promote together, open and strip tenants promote separately; regional malls have a common theme, open and strip centers are a collection of individual stores; regional malls can be crowded, forcing your customers to park some distance away, while open and strip centers hopefully provide parking at the door of the store.

Rents for the most part are not as high as in the regional covered malls. The competition for the available space is less and in most cases the landlord is willing to do more to secure and keep a tenant. He may offer more in the way of financial aid in original construction costs. Of course, all of this depends on the landlord's rate of occupancy.

The *small-store-as-parasite* thesis does not apply here; the traffic is considerably less since usually there is no major store from which to feed. However, because of the lower cost of operation, making a profit can be easier, and in the end that's what it's all about.

As a tenant in an *open* or *strip* center, you can set your own store hours. In a regional covered mall you may be tied to the hours set by the major stores. Most regional malls have a clause in their leases making it mandatory to have the smaller store's hours coincide with those of the major stores. In many instances this could mean late hours five or six nights per week. If this were the case, it would require extra help, greater utility bills, and mean an overall increase in your cost of operation. In the open and strip centers, this is usually not a cause for concern.

Making the Decision

Much of the decision as to the size of the center you choose is reached by the answer to the following questions:

1. How much capital do I have?
2. What price lines will I maintain? (A store dealing in expensive merchandise with a limited clientele does not require a great deal of traffic other than that which the store itself generates and therefore does not need the regional-type center as much as a store carrying more moderate priced goods does.)
3. Will the unique approach my store takes generate enough interest for my survival?
4. Can I live with only small stores to keep me company?

5. What are the shopping habits of the customers I hope to attract?
6. What is the size of the town in which I plan to open? (Large cities afford more opportunities for choice. Very small towns are not able to support a large regional mall and, therefore, all of the above is academic.)

When deciding which type of center is best for you, never listen to free advice. It is worth exactly what it costs. Check out the center for yourself. There are two good tests:

1. Talk to other *small* merchants in the center. They will usually give you an honest opinion. Talk to several in your industry and evaluate the persons with whom you are talking. You can tell if they are knowledgeable and if you should lean on what they say. Note that I say "in your industry" when selecting someone with whom to discuss the center. The reason for this is that what may be good for one type of store may not be good for another.

2. Clock the traffic in the center. This simply means visit the center at various times on different days and see if the mall and the stores are busy. Obviously, if you check a major store on Saturday afternoon, you will be viewing the world through rose-colored glasses. Check a small store on Tuesday at 11 A.M. or Wednesday at 4:30 P.M.. You will get the message quickly enough. And do it more than once—you could have hit them at a bad time. Remember when clocking that the weather is a factor. Snow and rain have a definite relationship to the traffic flow.

Since you have now decided on the type of center you require or can afford, your next big hurdle is dealing with the landlord to get the best possible lease your size operation deserves.

Remember, you are not Macy's, so don't expect to be treated like Macy's. With this rule firmly planted in mind, let's tackle the landlord and enter the world of bargaining, small print, aggravation, demands, leases, cooperation, and——hopefully—many years of a pleasant relationship.

Four

The Lease
and the Landlord

*It's like marriage . . .
a piece of paper and you belong to each other.*

Primary Considerations

I toyed with the thought of entitling this chapter "Friend or Foe" but cast this idea aside in favor of "The Lease and the Landlord." However, the difference is a matter too small to discuss.

When you have answered all the questions in the preceding chapter and know exactly where you want to open your store, the next problem facing you is the lease.

Primary Rule 1

Know what you are signing! Just because they hand you a pen doesn't mean you have to sign. If you learn nothing else from this book, let it be this: understand *everything* you sign —before you sign it!

Remember, leases were made for reading and understanding, not just for signing. Anyone can sign anything put in front of him, but a good businessperson will read, understand, comprehend all the hidden facets, discuss, negotiate, and then—all meeting with approval—sign.

As we said in the very beginning, a lease is like marriage—a piece of paper and you belong to each other. Make sure you can live together.

Primary Rule 2

All leases are written by lawyers, and therefore only lawyers can read them. The cheapest and best money you will spend will be the attorney's fee for reading the lease. Remember, what you sign will marry you to the landlord for three to five years or more. In the business world, unlike society at large, we have not seen a change whereby you can live with the landlord for a few years and then, if you are compatible—marry. We live in a very old-fashioned (commercial) world—marry first, and if you don't like it, get a divorce at the end of the lease. This can, of course, get expensive.

Primary Rule 3

A lease is written for the benefit of the landlord. Never lose sight of the fact that you are playing the game on his field, by his rules, and with his ball. There is much to be said for the home court advantage.

Do not be misled by the above statement into thinking that all leases are oppressive and unfair. The landlord wants you to be successful and prosper. Based on the type of lease you sign (some call for a percentage of sales), the better you do, the more income the landlord can realize from his property.

Here we should explain the percentage lease. A percentage lease simply means that after your base rent has covered minimum sales, you pay a percentage of all net sales over that minimum.

Example: You have a 5 percent lease with a $100,000 sales base. Your monthly rent will be $500. Once you exceed $100,000 in sales, you pay a 5 percent bonus to the landlord of all sales over $100,000. If you do $120,000, then you owe the landlord $1000, or 5 percent of $20,000. I always hoped to be in percentage rent since at that point I knew my rent was frozen at 5 percent of sales.

If, based on the above formula, you did only $80,000 (remember your base rent stays at $500 per month) then your rent would be 7.5 percent. The figures I have used are for example only, since actual percentages vary from city to city and center to center.

With the above in mind, you still must understand all provisions and clauses in the lease. These are the rules by which the game is played. Remember all games are played by rules, and if you don't know the rules you can't play the game. Aside from the obvious items found in a lease such as rent, term of the lease, location, and percentage (if any), there are other provisions, of which you may not be aware.

Other Provisions of Your Lease

Utilities

Who pays them—you or the landlord? If paid by you, are they paid directly to the utility company on an independent meter? Do you pay the landlord, who has billed you on a pro-rated share of the entire center based on square footage? Does the landlord request, or require, that you leave your front door open (so that your air conditioning services the common mall area)? Remember, if you pay utility bills to the landlord on a prorated share, you may be paying him a markup on the amount you actually use. Over the period of a lease this can add up to a considerable amount of money.

Store Hours

Are you tied to the opening and closing time of the center, or, more particularly, of a major store? As we discussed in

Chapter 3: a lease in a regional mall may require that the smaller stores maintain business hours to coincide with the major stores so that the mall will open and close uniformly.

Tax Increase

Is there a clause requiring you to pay your prorated share of tax increases levied against the entire center after you sign your lease? (The reason I say *after* you sign your lease is that it is normal to use the date of your lease as the base tax period.) If increases in the tax base occur after that date, you are responsible for your prorated share.

Merchants Associations

Are you required to join a merchants association composed of all the tenants? I neither commend or condemn this type of group. They serve a purpose when directly involved in a cooperative advertising program that can promote traffic in the center. You must always keep in mind that your association dues are the same as "rent" and must be considered in your overall cost of operations.

I have been involved with many of these types of groups. They generally fall into two types, both of which charge you a fee based on the square footage of your store.

Group I: The active group, promoting the center and generally with a gung-ho merchant as president. It takes its job seriously and promotes the center to the benefit of all. This type of group usually charges a monthly fee and operates within a budget.

Group II: This group charges no monthly fee but assesses each member his prorated share to pay for individual promotions. This group usually comes to life only at Easter and Christmas and usually does not have dynamic leadership.

Common Area Fee

This is another one of those expenses that must be considered as part of the rent. It is usually used for the maintenance of the mall itself. This charge is not generally found outside the large covered regional center.

Parking Area Fee

Like merchant association and common area fees, this one can add to your overall cost and should be considered part of the rent. This fee means just what it says: it is used for the maintainance of the parking lot.

Repairs

In most leases the tenant is responsible for the care and upkeep of the premises with the exception of the roof and outside walls. One of the exceptions to this rule is for water damage done to your portion of the premises through the landlord's roof. If this happens and should ruin your interior fixtures, merchandise, or carpeting, you can look to the landlord for relief. This is generally true in all types of centers.

Special Promotions

Be careful to know before you sign if you can be assessed a fee (usually prorated) for special events to be run by the center jointly by all the tenants. In most cases, this matter is handled through the merchants association and not by an extra assessment. No one is saying that you should not participate in functions that benefit the center, but be aware that these charges can appear, so don't be surprised if they do.

Landlord Participation

In some cases the landlord will participate financially in events that help promote the center. This, too, is done in conjunction with the merchants association.

The landlord can, and often does, participate in the cost of *finishing* in addition to the three walls and concrete slab mentioned before. The landlord will, on occasion, allow you so much per square foot toward finishing the interior of the store. This allowance will in no way pay for all your costs—it will not even pay for half—but something is better than nothing. An old rule is: any stipend offered, take!

If this stipend can be garnered from the landlord, there are two ways to collect: (1) upon completion of the work, the landlord gives you a check, (2) collect part as you complete portions of the job. The second way is the preferable of the two, since you are using his money as you go along. The less you have to finance, the less interest you have to pay as I have said previously.

Opening Date

The landlord should adhere to a specified opening date for the entire center and not open it piecemeal. This, of course, applies only when going into a new center. It is not uncommon for the major store or stores to open first and then the smaller stores and the connecting mall. There is little you as a small tenant can do about this situation, but you can insist on an opening date for the center's *grand opening*, to be spelled out in your lease agreement.

Signs

A very important clause. Some centers require all signs (store names) to be the same size and type of lettering. This eliminates any chance of personal identification. If at all possible, you should be permitted to use your own logo (style of lettering). But if the entire center is adhering to this rule, you cannot change it.

Restrictions on the size and use of paper signs can be harmful. I have seen leases that forbid the use of paper signs attached to the window glass—a rule that can make your life difficult, especially when you are running a sale.

It might prove wise to have the above, plus other items, in a lease negotiated by your attorney. Some can be eliminated, some altered, and some you will just have to live with.

Dealing with Owners, Agents, Landlords

Owners and leasing agents of large regional centers are more difficult to deal with when trying to get concessions. If it is a successful center, they usually have more than one prospective tenant vying for the space you want and they can afford to be more independent. If the center is large, but not successful, and has several vacancies from which to choose, you may want to investigate it more carefully (and possibly pass it up no matter how good the deal). *Cheap is cheap!*

Landlords of stores in strip or open centers are for the most part not big operators, as are the owners of the regional covered malls, and they are usually more accessible. This is by no means to suggest that they are an easy mark, but only that they will be easier to talk to.

Human nature being what it is, every landlord feels his property is a diamond, and will try to merchandise it to what he considers its fullest value. What you consider "its fullest value" will be based on different criteria. You must, at all times, never lose sight of the fact that if you pay too much rent (based on estimated sales), you can end up working for the landlord instead of yourself. "Working for the landlord" simply means that profits that you could otherwise be making are going to the landlord in the form of too much rent.

In the course of operating my business I had stores in both regional malls and open and strip centers. I found it generally true that I never saw or met the owner of the large regional mall in which I was a tenant. My dealings were strictly with his leasing agent or mall manager. I usually knew the owner of the open or strip center. We were on a first-name basis and occasionally had lunch together. Problems were more easily solved.

The information just discussed is a generalization. Never forget you are dealing with human nature. The relationship between landlord and tenant, once you get the formalities out of the way, are still based on such factors as personality, impressions, and chemistry. I had one open-center owner who was difficult. He made assurances he either had no intention of keeping, or could not fulfill. On the other hand, we were in a large regional mall where the resident mall manager went "that extra step" to keep his tenants happy.

Let me repeat: talk to your lawyer and accountant. They should be used as sounding-boards and even crutches, but the final decision must be yours.

You have already taken on both the center and the landlord; now all you have to do is come up with the money. Accordingly, the next chapter deals with financing.

Five

Financing

*A penny here and a penny there
and before you know it you have two cents.*

How Much Initially?

The financing of a business starts long before you are ready to open your front doors and begin doing business. Unless you had a rich uncle who left you a fortune (and if that is the case, why are you opening a store?) then your *initial* capital plus *operating* capital must be arranged for before you can even start. This before-the-fact money is called *cash reserves* or *investment dollars*, and would seem to prove the old adage that it takes money to make money.

The question most frequently asked by people considering going into business is, "How much money should I have before going into business?" or, to put it another way, "How much on-hand cash should I have to cover initial expenses?"

There is no pat dollar-and-cents answer to this question. There is no way to tell you the exact amount you will need without first knowing all the facts pertaining to your particular store. There are, however, certain rules of thumb to consider:

1. Research your fixed expenses. A *fixed expense* is that cost of operation which will remain the same regardless of the sales generated (i.e. rent, utilities, insurance, mall charges, etc.). The amount you arrive at should cover the first eighteen months of operation. This, of course, is a *"guesstimation,"* but you can come close.
2. Now do the same *"guesstimating"* for those expenses over which you do have some control (i.e. cost of goods, cost of supplies, salaries, advertising, display, etc.). Use the same period of time for these calculations.
3. Put steps 1 and 2 together and they spell the money you will be required to spend. Whatever figure you arrived at, increase it at least 10 percent because you have probably figured too low.
4. Now that you have guessed at your fixed expenses and your not-so-fixed expenses, take a guess at how much money you estimate your business will generate. I told you to increase your amount since you probably figured too low; now reverse it and decrease the income by 10 percent because you probably figured too high.

The SBA Loan

Banks and the government are two sources of money; neither is easy. The government has programs available through the Small Business Administration—known as the *SBA Loan*. Your lawyer or accountant will be familiar with this agency and can advise you on the proper steps to be taken. However, here is a brief review of the SBA.

The Small Business Administration (or SBA as we will call it from now on) is the first U.S. Government Agency to be established during peacetime, the only purpose of which is to assist and advise the small businessperson. The agency was created by the Small Business Act of 1953 and made permanent with expanded authority and responsibilities by the Small Business Act of 1958.

The SBA has many programs for your assistance including technical, procurement, research, management, investment (long-term money needs) and financial (short-term money needs). As with all government agencies, the SBA is head-quartered in Washington, D.C., but has about 100 field offices located in many of the nation's largest industrial and commercial cities. These local offices have been delegated decision-making authority to provide quick service.

The definition of a small business has changed over the years. From time to time the SBA has raised the amount of dollar volume (currently it is $2–7.5 million receipts) and number of employees you may employ. If you are opening a small store the fact that they raise the limits will have little importance. You should qualify if you meet their other requirements.

The SBA serves the business community in many ways. One of the most important is in the area of financial aid to small business people when loans are not readily obtainable elsewhere at reasonable rates. There are two primary avenues offered by SBA: *Participation Loans* and *Direct Loans*. Participation loans are loans made by the SBA (up to 90%) in conjunction with a bank or lending institution. By law, the SBA may not make a loan to you directly if you can get the money from a bank or other lending institution. Therefore, you must make application in the private sector (as opposed to the government sector) before applying to the agency. If you live in a city of 200,000 people or more, you must apply to two banks or lending institutions in the private sector before applying directly to the SBA for a loan.

To qualify for an SBA loan, the applicant must meet certain requirements set forth by the SBA's loan policy board:

1. The applicant must be of good character.
2. The applicant must show evidence of having the ability to run a business successfully.
3. The applicant must have enough money already invested in their business so that the SBA loan will be the additional

money needed to put the operation on solid financial footing.
4. As required by the Small Business Act, the loan "must be of
   such a sound value or so secured as reasonably to assure
   repayment."
5. The agency must have reasonable assurance that the business
   will be able to repay any borrowed money out of income
   from the business.
6. The applicant must agree to all SBA regulations that there
   will be no discrimination in employment or services to the
   public, based on race, color, religion, national origin, or
   marital status.

The SBA offers many additional loan plans. The following
are some of the loans and services available as they appear in
SBA Booklet OPI-6, *SBA: What It Does.*

Other SBA Financial Assistance and Loans

Regular Business Loans

Under Section 7(a) of the Small Business Act, as amended,
SBA is authorized to make regular business loans to small
firms on a direct, participation, or guaranteed basis.

Economic Opportunity Loans

The Agency grants Economic Opportunity Loans to help
persons who are *socially or economically disadvantaged* own
their own businesses. Both prospective and established small
firms are eligible for these loans.

State Development Company Loans

State Development Companies, which are organized by a
specific act of a state legislature to assist state-wide business
growth and development including small business growth,
may apply for SBA State Development Company Loans.
These monies are then used to supply small business concerns
within the state with long-term loans and equity capital.

Handicapped Assistance Loans

Physically handicapped small business owners and public and private nonprofit organizations which employ, and operate in the interests of, physically handicapped persons are eligible for Handicapped Assistance Loans.

Physical Damage Natural Disaster Recovery Loans

When the President or the Administrator of SBA declares a specific geographical area a disaster area as a result of a natural disaster, such as a hurricane, a widespread fire, a tornado, flooding, earthquake, etc., homeowners, renters, and the owners of small and large businesses within the disaster area may apply to SBA for home, personal property, and business Disaster Recovery Loans to repair or replace damaged or destroyed property.

Economic Injury Natural Disaster Loans

When the President, the Secretary of Agriculture, or the Administrator of SBA declares a specific geographical area a disaster area as a result of a natural disaster, the owners of small businesses which have suffered economic losses as a result of the disaster may apply to SBA for Economic Injury Loans for working capital and funds to pay financial obligations which the owners could have met if the disaster had not occurred.

Base Closing Economic Injury Loans

Base Closing Economic Injury Loans are made to small firms which have suffered, or will suffer, substantial economic injury as a result of the closing of a major federal military installation or a severe reduction in the scope and size of operation of a major military installation. These loans can be used to help a small business continue in business at its existing location, reestablish its business, purchase a new business, or establish a new business.

Management Assistance

As we said in Chapter 1, more businesses fail because of poor management than from any other cause. SBA recognizes this fact and in addition to financial assistance offers:

Counseling

SBA helps small business owners obtain individual assistance with management problems, and counsels prospective small business owners who want management information on specific types of business enterprises.

SCORE/ACE and Professional Association Volunteers

In addition to the help provided by SBA Management Assistance staff, management counseling can be obtained from the members of the *Service Corps of Retired Executives/Active Corps of Executives* (SCORE/ACE) and numerous national professional associations, all of whom have volunteered to help prospective small business owners and troubled small businesses. SBA tries to match the need of a specific small business with the expertise of one of its thousands of volunteers. The assigned counselor visits the small business in question. Through careful observation, a detailed analysis is made of the business and its problems. If the problems are complex, the counselor may call on other volunteer experts to help the small business. Finally, a plan is offered to remedy the trouble and assist the business through its critical period.

Small Business Institute (SBI)

Through the Small Business Institute, senior and graduate students of the nation's leading schools of business provide on-site management counseling to small business owners.

The students are guided by a faculty member and an SBA Management Assistance Officer, and they receive academic credit for their participation in the Institute. Although SBI counseling is usually restricted to SBA clients (loan recipients and small firms performing federal contracts), it is available if there are enough student counselors in the program to assist all small business owners who want SBI help.

Courses

Business management courses concerning planning, organizing, and controlling a business, as distinguished from day-to-day operating activities, are co-sponsored by SBA and public and private educational institutions and business associations. The courses are generally held during the evening, and last from six to eight weeks.

Conferences, Workshops, and Clinics

Conferences covering subjects such as working capital, business forecasting, and diversification of markets are held for established businesses on a regular basis. SBA also conducts Pre-Business Workshops dealing with capital requirements, sources of financing, types of business, business organization, and business site selection for prospective small business owners. Clinics concerning specific problems of small firms in specific industrial categories are held on an as-needed basis.

Publications

SBA issues hundreds of management, technical, and marketing publications which have been valuable aids to millions of established or prospective managers of small firms. Most of these management publications are available from the Agency, free of charge, while others can be obtained for a small fee from the Superintendent of Documents at the U.S.

Government Printing Office in Washington, D.C. In addition to management assistance publications, brochures explaining each of the Agency's areas of assistance are available at all SBA offices.

Minority Small Business

SBA has combined its efforts with those of private industry, banks, local communities, and other Federal agencies to increase substantially the number of small businesses which are owned and operated by citizens who are members of socially or economically disadvantaged minority groups. In addition to the Economic Opportunity Loan Program . . . the Agency's overall Minority Small Business Program brings all of SBA's services together in a coordinated effort to make more sound business opportunities available to socially and economically disadvantaged individuals. A Minority Small Business Overview Staff located in the Agency's Washington, D.C., Central Office is assisted by Minority Small Business field representatives stationed in SBA's ten regional offices and many district offices. Minority Small Business staff members cooperate with local business development organizations and explain to potential minority entrepreneurs how SBA's services and programs can help them become successful business owners.

Advocacy

SBA actively and forcefully represents the small business community at national, state, and local government levels and with business, professional, and trade associations and organizations. The Agency's Advocacy Office endeavors to find out what problems small businesses are having, calls these problems to the attention of Government officials, and attempts to develop solutions to these problems. SBA is the focal point for complaints, criticisms, and suggestions from small businesses about other Federal departments. SBA and the Advocacy Office counsels individual small business owners and groups of small firms on the best ways to resolve their difficulties with such problems as the burden of complying with Government regulations, paperwork requirements, and product liability.

Women In Business

Prospective and established women business owners are eligible for all of SBA's programs and services. The Agency understands the unique problems faced by women in business and is on constant alert to see that special attention is given to them. All too many women in business who need help are not coming to SBA for assistance, and the Agency has started a major National Outreach Program to encourage more women to apply for SBA's services and start businesses of their own.

Help for Veterans of the Armed Forces

Veterans of the Armed forces...[have] specifically designated SBA Veterans Affairs Officers [to] assure that veterans receive the benefits of all of the programs the Agency provides and that special consideration is given to veterans and their survivors and dependents.

All of the areas of SBA participation we have covered so far are just some of the activities of this government agency. If you decide to take advantage of the opportunities offered by the SBA to new store openings, here are eight steps you must follow:

1. Describe in detail the type of business to be established.
2. Describe experience and management capabilities.
3. Prepare an estimate of how much you and others have to invest in the business and how much you need to borrow.
4. Prepare a current financial statement (balance sheet) listing all personal assets and all liabilities.
5. Prepare a detailed projection of earnings for the first year the business will operate.

6. List collateral to be offered as security for the loan, indicating your estimate of the present market value of each item.
7. Take this material with you and see your banker. Ask for a direct bank loan and, if declined, ask the bank to make the loan under SBA's Loan Guaranty Plan or to participate with SBA in a loan. If the bank is interested in an SBA guaranty or participation loan, ask the banker to contact SBA for discussion of your application. In most cases of guaranty of participation loans, SBA will deal directly with the bank.
8. If a guaranty or a participation loan is not available, write or visit the nearest SBA office. SBA has 96 field offices and, in addition, sends loan officers to visit many smaller cities on a regularly scheduled basis or as the need is indicated. To speed matters, make your financial information available when you first write or visit SBA.

Your Accountant

As I have said before, "talk to your accountant." Let me stop here and talk about *your accountant*. There are accountants and there are accountants. In today's world of specialization, we have accountants who specialize in different areas for different industries. If you are opening a small apparel store, you shouldn't have an accountant who has done all of his postgraduate work on the care and feeding of oil leases. He should be familiar with, and understand, the problems of your particular type of retailing. And your particular type of retailing is a *small store*.

Accountants have been said "to speak the language of business." If the language of business is to take the facts and daily transactions of commerce and collect, classify, and relate them to management in an orderly manner based on accounting principles and procedures, and in accounting terms, you had best understand what they are trying to say.

Do not be overwhelmed by pages of numbers and the process that generates their final form. Accountants go to school for many years to learn the process. Your job is to know what they mean.

Accounting is more than a dull routine of collecting numbers and putting them down on paper in a prescribed order. Your accountant must be able to think and communicate. He must be able to recognize a problem (before it becomes insurmountable), think it through to a logical conclusion, and explain it to you in such a way that proper steps can be taken to correct the situation.

Fees are negotiable! You cannot afford to pay what the big boys pay, yet you must have someone upon whom you can lean when the time arises. In the beginning, you must have someone to guide you through the economic jungle, or you will be eaten by the lion of uncontrolled expenses or the tiger of bad management.

What all this means is that just because cousin Clyde studied accounting does not necessarily mean that he is good for your business. He may be charming and witty, and your mother may be pushing you to use him, but don't weaken if he is wrong for you; pass!

Getting back to financing: our discussion of SBA loans raises the subject of banks.

Your Banker

The old adage that banks love to loan money to people who don't need the money isn't necessarily wrong, but it's not altogether true, either. Seriously, it pays to have a friendly banker. Here, as with your accountant and lawyer, shop around. Not all banks offer the same services, and not all loan officers are alike (some are tougher). Remember, banks are in business to make money, and the only commodity they have to sell is money itself. When you ask for a loan, you are, in reality, asking them to give you money in exchange for a piece of paper from which they are to collect their debt. Do not confuse their cautiousness with a hardheaded attitude.

If you listen to bank commercials on television you will be led to believe that biggest is best, first is best, the neighborhood bank is best, small is best, etc., etc., etc.—hogwash! The best is the one that is best for *you*. When you get past the rhetoric, you will find that you will lean on your accountant and lawyer, and on your own personal instincts based on shopping the money market, before choosing a banker.

At this juncture there are many questions about any banker you are considering that should be asked. Does the bank have a reputation for being progressive? What are its loan policies when compared to the other banks in your city? Will it grant you loans large enough to accomplish your ends? How do its loan officers approach your problems? Are you comfortable with them when discussing your needs? Do they *seem* friendly?

If you think a bank is just a building to hold your deposits, permit you to write checks against those funds, and send you a monthly statement, then all you require is the bank located nearest your store. Using the above criteria, your choice of a banker is easy.

If, however, you are going to need loan assistance, financial advice, someone to talk with about your business problems, what's going on in your industry, establishing a good credit rating for the marketplace, then you should choose your banker very carefully.

Taking the questions we originally asked (three paragraphs back), let's examine them for answers:

A Progressive Reputation

There is more to being a progressive institution than the type of furniture they use, whether plastic or marble prevails, the location of their drive-through windows, the kinds of prizes used for opening new accounts, how cool the air conditioning is kept, etc.

A progressive bank should have both the vitality of youth and the experience that comes from maturity. Your banker should be young enough to still be excited by the birth of a new small business and old enough to give you advice based on having been down that road before. Your banker and the bank should be involved in matters affecting the community as a whole.

Has your business been actively sought by an officer of the bank or does the bank seem to expect your account as a matter of course? Is the bank truly "full service" (e.g.: bank-by-mail, personal loans, installment credit for small businesses, low-cost personal checking accounts, night depositories, etc.) or just a thirty-second commercial on TV? Speaking of TV commercials, this can be a test of a bank's progressiveness: are its ads catchy and entertaining, or do they use all the old banking clichés and bromides?

When we get down to the nitty-gritty, a bank is only as progressive as its officers. When meeting with your banker, much can be gleaned from their grasp of your problems and their attitude toward you and your business. Consider the *type of questions* they ask rather than merely concentrating on the answers. If they seem truly interested in you and your business and want to be of as much help as they can, this will be an important factor in determining which bank you choose.

What Are Bank Loan Policies?

Even though the lending policies of banks vary with each institution (and sometimes between officers within the same bank) the fundamental principles of bank loans remain the same.

Assuming that one of the traditional functions of a bank is to loan money to their commercial customers, then you as a prospective borrower must be prepared to furnish your loan officer information and assurances.

After we get past the basic information (like your name and address), your banker has to know just what size loan you will require. This is not as simple a question as it might seem at first reading. This figure is arrived at after a complete analysis of your business. Most people borrowing money will ask for more than is required to open and maintain their operation until the store's normal cash flow takes over.

All bankers must have verifiable data relating to your business and, in some cases, to you personally. If you are the kind of person who feels a tinge of resentment when asked for identification when cashing a personal check, then do not ask for a bank loan. For a bank loan, be prepared to bare your soul. Any banker worth his vice-presidency will want (and rightly so) a good deal of information upon which to base approval of your loan application. Remember, the more secure your loan is, the more the banker is doing his job of protecting you, the bank, and the depositors (to say nothing of his own job security). When he is finished asking questions, he should understand your needs better than you do.

I said above that the loan policies will include information and assurance. Let us now look at what assurances your banker will want. He must feel reasonably secure that you will repay your loan within the time frame of the loan agreement, and that the store you are planning to open will be a profitable operation.

Although the following is not a loan policy in the truest sense of the word, there are certain unwritten laws of behavior (or policies if you prefer) that all reputable bankers will adhere to: whatever you tell your banker will be held in absolute confidence. As with your lawyer, accountant, doctor, or clergyman, what you say is between just the two of you. If you have any doubts about his integrity, get another banker.

What we have discussed above are consistencies in loan policies between banks. Let us now take a look at the variances.

1. One bank may require collateral, while another may approve the loan on your signature.
2. One bank may require you to maintain a certain balance

(usually a percentage of the loan), while the second bank will have no such requirement.
3. One bank may charge a small interest on the unused portion of a "revolving-credit" or standby reserve account, while another bank may have no such charge.
4. The first bank may require a co-signer, while the second bank will not.
5. One bank's officers may offer financial advice and counsel, while another bank's officers cannot or will not.
6. The first bank may permit overdrafts (another means of loaning money without a separate formal agreement), while the other bank would "bounce" your checks.

One rule always to remember when borrowing money from a bank is that their one overriding policy is: Banks prefer loaning money to people who do not really need it or could almost get along without it.

Does the Bank Grant Large Enough Loans?

Because you are a small merchant, your loan requirements will not be as large as your banker is used to seeing. To you they will seem high, but to them the amount will be moderate to small. It is at this point that your personal relationship with your banker and his understanding of your business and its problems become vital to the wellbeing of your operation.

In these days of high interest rates and complicated federal regulations, bankers must be very discriminating in the matter of with whom they place their available loan funds. It may therefore become more difficult for them to open new accounts.

There are services offered by banks of which you should be aware. Do they offer "term loans"? Do they factor accounts receivable? Do they advance against furniture and fixtures? Are they large enough for all your needs? These are all questions (and your accountant can think of more) that you should be able to answer before affiliating.

You should know that bank loans come in all shapes and sizes. Just as you would not stock a store with nothing but size 10 dresses or all size Small shirts, so banks carry a *run of sizes* in their loan inventory.

Loans can be:

(1) straight 30- to 90-day,

(2) installment with set monthly payments,

(3) secured (and, in some rare cases, unsecured) term loans running from one to ten years,

(4) accounts receivable loans, whereby you sign over the title of your accounts receivable as collateral,

(5) loans wherein you use your inventory and/or the furniture and fixtures as security, and

(6) a (not-so) simple loan where you put up almost everything you own: (personal property, cash value on life insurance policies, stocks, etc.) as the loan guarantee.

What Is the Loan Officer's Approach?

In addition to all I have said, your loan officer must be competent, knowledgeable, and friendly. Any one of the above without the others is not good enough. A banker must have all three.

When we speak of a loan officer's *approach*, we mean this in the broadest possible sense. An approach is not *your first meeting* but the way the officer handles your needs over the years of your relationship. It is constant consultation and very much a two-way street. If you do not keep him informed of fluctuations in your business, then he cannot advise you intelligently.

Although you may feel perfectly secure in running your business yourself, it is always good to have someone to "bounce problems off of" such as your loan officer. And remember, keep the relationship on a plane that will make it profitable to you both. Just as when you go to market you have a general idea of what you are going to buy, so should you know your needs when you approach your banker.

I once knew a store owner who was awed by banks and bankers. Remember, banks are merely *stores* where you, as a customer, intend to make a purchase. Just as you do not sell every shopper who walks through your front door, neither do bankers make every loan they would like to. If they do not have what you need, shop elsewhere.

Loan Agreements

When borrowing money from a bank, there are certain pitfalls to avoid if at all possible. Remember that all *loan agreements* (like leases for the landlord) are written for the bank's protection—not yours. *Make sure, before you sign, that you understand everything you are signing.* Two of the major items to be considered are:

How You Sign

If, on advice of your accountant, you have formed a corporation, then sign as a corporation. All lenders will try for a *personal* signature. Be sure you understand what this means and all the possibilities it presents. A personal signature means exactly what it says: you are *personally* responsible for any and all debts incurred by the company. Depending on the laws of your state, your creditors can levy against all of your personal property in case of default on the loan. Lenders have an old barb they sometimes use with borrowers who balk at signing personally: "If *you* don't have faith in your business, why should *we*?" Don't be intimidated by this ploy. They are getting paid to have faith. If you sign as an officer of the corporation, only the business can be held responsible for the debts of the business.

The "Mother Hubbard" Clause

If you remember the nursery rhyme, Old Mother Hubbard had a cupboard that was bare. In banking circles, a Mother Hubbard clause means that if you default on a loan, the bank can take all the money you have anywhere in that bank and apply it against the balance owing on the loan, leaving your "cupboard" bare.

Let me explain Mother Hubbard this way: If you owe the bank $10,000 and you have $2,000 in your checking account, and you cannot meet your loan payment, the bank can *offset* your checking account and apply the $2,000 against your loan, leaving a balance of $8,000. At this point, you still owe the remainder of the loan and can't pay any other bills because the bank took all the money in your checking account. In defense of the bank, it should be said that this is usually a last-ditch effort on its part to recoup some of what you owe, since it is obvious that your chances of staying in business are poor. Of course, sometimes an *off-set* can make those chances zero.

The reason I bring up this clause is for you to be aware of what can happen, so that nothing comes to you as a surprise. If you can't get this clause struck out of the loan agreement, it behooves you to have another account in a different bank. A Mother Hubbard clause is good only at the lending bank, and that bank cannot off-set an account in another bank. All of this is almost academic, since it is difficult (if not impossible) to have this clause taken out, and most banks require that you keep your checking account with them if they are to lend you money. The second account of which I spoke would be for surplus funds.

There are many other factors to consider when obtaining loans (either from conventional lending institutions or the government) and *none should be attempted without the advice of your accountant.*

There is always the option of borrowing from friends and relatives. This is to be used only as a last resort. Polonius wasn't so wrong when he said in Act 1, Scene 3, of Hamlet, "Never a borrower, nor lender be; for loan oft loses both itself and friend . . . ." It's a good idea to listen to Shakespeare and stick with the normal money sources.

Six

Expenses

In America,
it's not how much an item costs,
it's how much you save!

This is the single most important part of your operation. It is here, in a day-to-day struggle, that a business can succeed or go down the tubes.

For the most part, expenses govern cash. There is more to "cash" than what the Federal Government mints or prints. Cash as we discuss it here is basically divided into two categories, *capital* and *working*. It is vital that you, as a small business operator, know the difference between *capital* and *working cash* and that you make no mistake about how to handle each.

Capital and Working Cash
(Cash Flow)

Capital-type cash is sometimes referred to as *capital invest-ment*. This simply means the monies spent for fixed assets (i.e. fixtures, furniture, investments, earned and retained profits, and reserves for depreciation). These items will appear on your balance sheet, which we will discuss at greater length in Chapter 12 on record-keeping.

Working capital is the monies spent on merchandise, sup-plies, advertising, window trims, etc. The source of all work-ing cash is the profits from the operation of your store.

Working cash can also be called *"cash flow."* This term, like so many, means exactly what it says: the flow of cash through your business. As your sales produce cash, you pur-chase inventory and pay your overhead expenses. You sell the inventory, which again produces cash (or creates ac-counts receivable) with which to buy more inventory and pay more bills; this merry-go-round is known as your cash flow.

Each individual business has its own cash flow cycle. Good money management requires you to know the time frame in-volved in this cash-to-sales-to-cash flow and the amount of cash that you can expect to support your volume.

Cash Requirements Schedule

You can tell easily if your business is operating correctly in this cash cycle by doing a study of your flow and the timing of your cash. Taking your sales figures and subtracting your purchases and expenses should present you with a picture of how your business is using its cash. We can call this your *cash requirements schedule*.

The secret of a cash requirements schedule is *keep it simple*. Doing the study recommended above, you should have the actual amount spent, your actual cash needs, and your spending plan for a given period of time (i.e. week, month, or quarter). An annual forecast by months is common in most businesses. However, use the system best suited to your particular operation.

As I said, keep it simple. A cash requirements schedule does not have to be an elaborate bookkeeping system. A columnar sheet showing estimated sales (use last year's figures as a guide if you have any) in one column and expenses and purchases in another column will suffice.

Knowing the approximate amount of cash you will have determines the direction of the business. When you start on a long trip, it is important that you have a map. A map not only shows where you are but how far you have to go and the proper route to take. In business we have many maps to follow. The cash requirements schedule is but one.

Current Ratio

Cash flow can be described in yet another way: staying liquid or dry. It's not that difficult to stay liquid if you have this information at your fingertips. Without it you can wander down a dark alley which may, or may not, have a door out when you get to the end. All of this is to say, *if you aren't liquid, you can't pay you bills.* If you can't pay your bills you aren't in business. To know constantly if you are in a liquid position is your job as the owner. This can be accomplished by a device known as figuring your current ratio. Determining ratio is governed by a relatively simple formula: using information contained in your balance sheet (see Chapter 12), *divide your current assets by your current liabilities.*

Let us say the XYZ Company has assets of $200,000 and current liabilities of $100,000. Their ratio is thus 2 to 1. In today's business world, a 2-to-1 ratio is considered good. However, 3 to 1 (if you are a concerned owner) is better. An ounce of caution is better than a pound of crying, wringing hands, and rolling on the floor kicking your feet.

Acid-Test Ratio

If you wish information even more exact than the current ratio, you can always use the *acid-test ratio*. The difference here is you use *only truly liquid assets* (cash and receivables).

As we saw, the liabilities of the XYZ Company were $100,000. Let us now make the assets $125,000 for a ratio of 1.25 to 1. Using the acid-test, a ratio of 1 to 1 is considered good *if the company is in a solid position* with no foreseeable complications. As with the previous ratio, it is always better to allow yourself the additional edge; shoot for 2 to 1.

This discussion of ratio in a chapter on expenses is not just stuck here for lack of a better place to put it. Ratio is one of the most important pieces of information you have to determine your ability to pay bills. Failing to keep track of your liquidity can result in your going back to work for someone else. Macy's can make a mistake in this area and still live well, but a small business will find it hard to survive this kind of miscalculation.

Improving Your Ratio

I have now told you the dangers and pitfalls of a poor liquid position. Before you panic, there are several ways to improve your ratio:

1. Let more of your profits remain in the business. Put back more than you take out (at least while you're building).
2. Build your equity, particularly with cash. Invest surplus cash in anything that pays interest.
3. Bank loans are a natural increase to your current assets.

These three items are by no means the only way to increase your ratio. The point here is to keep the ratio in mind, and if it is not up-to-standard, do something to improve your position.

Expenses are broken down into categories—those that are fixed and over which you have little or no control, and those which, by prudent supervision, can make the difference between profit and loss. Let us dispose of those expenses over which you can exercise little, if any, control such as rent, taxes, depreciation, freight (to a degree), and government fees.

John Ruskin, the nineteenth-century English art critic, writer, and social reformer, was an astute observer of his times, and little did he realize that what he said then could have a bearing on today's world of business: "It's unwise to pay too much, but it's worse to pay too little. When you pay too much, you lose a little money—that is all. When you pay too little, you sometimes lose everything, because the thing you bought was incapable of doing the thing it was bought to do."

I have quoted Ruskin at the beginning of our discussion on expenses with a definite purpose in mind. I will be saying over and over, *shop for the best price when buying supplies or employing help*. Although we never want to overpay, sometimes cheap is not best, and the advice given some 80 years ago by John Ruskin can serve us well.

Payroll and Sales Help

Now let us discuss those expenses over which you *must* exercise control. The most common mistake most merchants make with regard to payroll is to employ the same, fixed, number of people regardless of the volume anticipated. Obviously, you don't need as many employees in February as you do in December. Your payroll should peak in direct relationship to your expected increase in sales.

Another common mistake is to hire the cheapest possible help you can get. Remember, cheap is cheap, and you get what you pay for. This is particularly true when speaking of help. If your operation includes only two or three salespeople, then pay more, but get the best you can find. They will earn their pay in the additional volume they do over and above their salaries.

When interviewing potential sales help, there are the obvious traits to look for: neatness, ability to communicate, and a willingness to work. What you should also look for, but what is often neglected, is their ability to bring customers from their previous jobs. This is known as having a *"book."* A salesperson without a book is only half a salesperson. We'll look closer at the hiring of salespeople in Chapter 11.

Nonselling help such as. cashiers, maids, and alteration people (depending on the size of your operation) are a *must* to have and an absolute must to control. For example, if you had two alteration people for Christmas and Easter and they were able to handle the workload, then one full-time—or even one part-time—person may suffice at other times of the year.

It is always easy to be a good guy and give people work— and very difficult to cut back or discharge inefficient people. However, you want to be a boss, and this is your job.

Bad Checks

This nemesis of the merchant is definitely an expense—a case of the *fast draw* being a disadvantage, rather than the edge: the faster you draw the money from the cash register (or cash drawer) or the faster you accept a check for a purchase, the faster you may lose money.

Over the years, certain perils of being in business have come and gone. Some assumed paramount importance only to fade as business conditions changed. Ever since banks began dispensing funds on a customer's signature, no peril has remained such a constant threat to your profits.

Never lose sight of the fact that taking a *"hot"* check is the same as giving the merchandise away. Once the customer walks through the door, you have lost all control over the goods. Apparel is not like furniture, jewelry, cars, or heavy appliances, whereby the store can obtain a "right of seques-tration" (the right to repossess). This is of little good when ap-plied to apparel. What are you going to do with used clothing?

The accepting of checks, without every proper precaution, is like going to Las Vegas with no conception of how the various games of chance operate. The chances of fraud or insufficient funds gang up on millions of small business people (and large ones too) for millions, if not billions, of dollars in losses each year.

Small businesses are an easier target than the large stores. Department stores have a rigidly adhered-to procedure that minor employees must observe. As an owner/manager, you will be more prone *not to lose the sale* or to *judge a person by his/her honest face*. This is a battle you must constantly fight. Do not let these two factors lull you into a sense of false security.

Don't let me talk you out of ever cashing or taking a personal check. There are several very simple procedures to follow, and if cashing checks becomes a matter of necessity, these procedures can make it profitable.

1. Identification: Require a valid driver's license and one major credit card. Social Security cards do not count.
2. Do not accept second-party checks.
3. Obtain home and business phone numbers.
4. The check should be for no more than the amount of the purchase.
5. When cashing a payroll check, it should be for a purchase or payment only. When doing this, subtract the amount purchased or paid from the amount of the check on the back of the check. This serves two purposes: (a) it acts later as identification of transaction, if needed, and (b) it may eliminate errors in making change.
6. Refuse any checks with altered numbers or signatures that do not look right to you. This is done on general principle and requires no explanation.
7. In addition to the above, there are various check-cashing protection services to which you can subscribe. These usually work by having a phone number to call and by feeding in a code number and the customer's driver's license number; you can get immediate approval or rejection.

These services will usually guarantee your losses up to a certain amount. However, you pay for this protection. It will probably be wise to start by doing your own thing. If by experience you find that your losses are running too high, you can always get this hired service.

Advertising and Display

I have lumped these two expenses together since they both are geared to do the same thing—that is, to get customers into the store. Since this expense varies with the season, it is wise to keep the cost to a percentage of expected sales. Note I said *expected* sales, since you must spend the money (or at least allocate the expense) before you have realized the sales to be generated. All businesses, based on their size, have set percentages for each expense item. I will cover this at greater length in a later chapter devoted solely to this item.

Dues and Subscriptions

This may seem like an inconsequential item, but it is easy to get over-subscribed to magazines and clubbed to death joining every organization in town.

Magazines and trade publications in the proper doses are your continuing education in your industry. It is physically and financially impossible to be in the marketplace on a day-to-day basis, so it takes constant reading to keep yourself abreast of what is currently going on. However, this education does not require 10 or 15 publications coming to you every week, or even every month. For openers, you won't have the time, nor the inclination, to read them all, so therefore be selective. Two or three magazines and a like number of trade papers will suffice.

Dues paid to civic groups can serve as one of your better forms of advertising. Your presence at a Rotary or Kiwanis luncheon or a meeting of the local women's club will act as a reminder to those in attendance that you are a part of the community and that they should support you. This is in no way meant to detract from the good work done by these various groups (with your dues), but to merely show you a side benefit of your membership. Here again, as with anything else, it can be overdone. You can't belong to *everything*, so be selective.

Insurance

This is an expense that can, and should, be controlled. As with your CPA and attorney, make sure that the person handling your insurance program has *your* best interests at heart. Every one of us has a relative or friend who sells insurance, and we would like to throw some business their way. Just make sure they are professional and understand *your* needs and requirements. Remember, you are buying their expertise as well as their personality. The ability to make you laugh now can cause you to cry later.

In addition to being a competent salesperson, your agent should represent a reliable insurance company. The coverage recommended by the agent should be tailored to the particular requirements of your business, and the company should be of sufficient size and reputation to pay claims.

The actual decision of what insurance your business may need should be a consensus of opinion by your agent, your lawyer, your banker, and your accountant. The many details involved in a purchase this important calls for the *expert* qualified in the technical aspects of business insurance—*your agent*. For income and estate tax you'll need your lawyer plus the sound financial advice of your accountant and banker. Of course, the final decision is yours!

Don't be lulled into thinking that all insurance programs are the same or that the cost is the same. There are many different types of insurance, with each doing a different job. There are some policies that you should not carry. Example:

plate glass insurance for your store front. I have found that to make the premiums economically feasible, you would have to lose one window or more a year—otherwise, the cost of the insurance exceeds the cost of replacing the glass yourself *Paying for the replacement glass is called carrying your own insurance.* There may be several items like this, so know your agent and be sure that he has *your* best interests at heart and is not just looking to sell another policy.

When considering an insurance program, you must realize what the various risks are to your business. These risks fall into different categories: damage to your property, damage to someone else's property, liability to both your customers and your employees, credit losses and death benefits in a partnership.

To protect yourself in the event that any of the above should occur, there are policies that can be written for fidelity (insuring against employee theft), forgery, workers compensation, general liability, automobile, burglary, accident, life and health, or the death of a partner. The proceeds from a *key man* (death of an executive) policy can be paid directly to the business or it can be used to buy the partner's share of the business from the family and heirs.

Once you have established a plan that you feel gives you all the coverage you need, it behooves you to have periodic reviews of the entire program. There are changes occuring all the time in the insurance field. The "Rock" is not a solid rock —but rather a bunch of stones held together by time and circumstance.

Just as many see their doctors once a year, their dentists twice a year, you should sit down with your insurance agent and discuss changes in rates, coverage, and the law. It is prudent that the plan be kept as current as possible; again, not all of the above policies are economically feasible to carry. This you will decide with the help of your advisers.

Telephones

You may think that you pay the same for phones and phone service as everyone else, but this is true only to an extent. The savings here come from how much service you demand. Remember, Ma Bell gives you nothing for nothing. Each instrument, each extension, each little light that lights up, each fancy style costs money!

Every day the phone company comes out with a different gimmick you think you can't live without. Well, you not only *can* live without it, but you should. Fifty cents to $1.50 per month extra can add up to an unnecessary expense and many dollars over the course of a year.

The phone company employs service representatives who will survey your store's needs and suggest the type of equipment best suited to your operation. Listen to them, digest what they have to say, and then make up your *own* mind. You may find that you do not need that extra instrument in the front of the store—that to save the extra charges, you can walk the 20 feet to the cash stand where a *necessary* phone is located. You may find that two lines can handle your volume calls as well as three lines. Give this expense thought when buying phone service, since it is definitely controllable.

I have spoken solely of the Bell System—as if they were the only phone company in town. There has been, in recent years, an influx of smaller and private phone companies. It may be worth your while to investigate them for savings. If you consider using a smaller phone service (and in this case *small* is not *really small*), then insist on references with whom you can discuss the costs and services that you are actually paying for and receiving. There are certain hidden costs in the other services such as extra charges for repair calls, line charges, etc. This is another of those "I'll investigate, compare, and *then* make up my mind" areas.

Do not pay your phone bill without checking out every call and service for which you have been charged. Don't be bashful—call the business office of the phone company if you have any doubts or questions. The phone bill, along with every other invoice you receive, should be checked for accuracy every month before you issue a check.

Utilities

Your control over gas, water, and electricity charges is limited, at best. A penny saved is still a penny earned.

Like death and taxes, a rise in utility costs is a sure thing. By limiting the use of these items, however, a savings can be realized. The cost of electricity is directly proportional to its use: turn off lights when they are not needed. *Stockrooms and window lights are the chief offenders.* Most window lights are on a time clock that automatically turns the lights on and off. By checking your traffic, you will know when your lights should be off, and by checking when it gets dark, you will know when your lights should come on. (This will vary with the season of the year.) If you can effect reductions of only an hour or so per day of your lights' burning time, you will realize a savings.

This, of course, applies only to stores that face the street. If your store is located in an enclosed mall, then the timing of your window lights is tied directly to that of your neighbors. You certainly do not want a dark store when all around you is bright. On the other hand, yours do not have to be the last lights burning in the center. There is no trick to knowing when the other stores have their time clocks set to go on and off—ask them!

Much of the above applies to the air conditioning. If you keep the temperature set to federal guidelines, you will not only conserve energy, but you can cut your bill considerably. This also applies to your gas bill in the winter.

Water is almost an uncontrollable expense. Here it is not so much a matter of *reduced use* to realize a reduction in cost, but more a matter of *not wasting*. A running commode costs money. Make repairs promptly on dripping toilets and faucets. You will make back the repair bill by the monies saved on the water bill.

Office and Store Supplies

Once again, *you must be a shopper*. It is a fact that not all office-supply firms sell their products for the same price. This holds true for the same *national label* products sold at different stores. By doing a little shopping around, you will be surprised at how much you can save. I keep talking about *shopping around* and I do not want you to think that you need to run all over town. Much of this *shopping* can be done on the phone or by salemen calling on you. Let your fingers do the walking.

Primary Rule 1

Never, but never, buy more than you need.

Primary Rule 2

Be careful of salesmen bearing discounts. You may save a few cents, or even a dollar or two, by buying a two-year supply of toilet paper, but the cost of money being what it is, you will be a loser in the long run. Overspending like this could be your undoing. A *half* case of adding machine tape will last you six months; then don't buy a case. Plain pencils or ballpoint pens work just as well as ones with your name imprinted on them. Paper clips, staples, rubber bands, etc., are probably cheaper in *limited* quantities, in the long run, than tieing up your money for an extended period of time.

Business forms are another area in which to exercise great

caution when ordering. As your business progresses, you may change your operation (or your thinking as to what you need), and old forms can become very expensive scratch pads.

Boxes and bags are a major expense item. Like everything else, the price varies from one vendor to another. I can't say too often—shop around! Everyone wants to sell you, but it's your money you're spending, so be careful.

In shopping the market, you may find it is cheaper to use a plastic garment bag rather than a box. Do not forget to count the cost of a hanger when comparing prices. On the other hand, a small *paper* sack will, in most cases, be less expensive than the same size bag in *plastic*.

Your logo printed on all bags and boxes costs more than a plain container. Here I feel the additional cost is justified, since this is a valid form of advertising and helps project the image of your store. (We will get into the importance of image at greater length in a later chapter.)

Salesbooks should contain no more than you absolutely need for your bookkeeping purposes. Your business forms supplier usually has a standard two-part sales slip (with or without tissue) that can be printed with your logo. It would be rare that you needed a specially designed salesbook. These standard salesbooks can be had in colors to match your store's theme. Here again, do not buy more than you need.

Hangers are a continuing expense. Between those you use for stock and break and those that are given away with a purchase, you will find that you are buying this item more often than almost any other supply. It is not necessary to keep thousands in reserve, as your supplier can (and should) supply your needs quickly from his inventory. Let *him* stock them—not you.

Note the difference between *stock* and *give-away* hangers. All hangers come in varying degrees of strength and price. The stronger the hanger, the more it usually costs. Stock hangers are stronger and nicer than the cheaper, less sturdy give-away hangers.

If you are giving the merchandise to the customer on a hanger in a plastic bag, you do not need to give him or her a stock hanger. Buy a cheaper hanger for this purpose and have your cashier or salesperson change hangers before putting the garment in the plastic bag. This can secure a substantial savings.

Some janitorial supplies may be better purchased from the supermarket, one at a time, than bought from a wholesaler who has minimum-order requirements. One bottle of mirror cleaner may last you six months, so why buy a case?

Light bulbs come in many sizes and prices and for many different uses. Use the proper bulb in the proper place. Be on guard and do not let yourself be led astray by guarantees and discounts, which in the long run can be more expensive.

Obviously I cannot cover every item you will have to buy in the way of supplies. If you have got nothing else from this chapter it should be: *shop around!* If you do this, you are ahead of the game. Also, never lose sight of the fact that shopping is an ongoing process. Do not become married to one supplier, but periodically shop the market to make sure that your supplier still offers the best deal in town. Never accept an increase in cost on any supply item without shopping your supplier's competitors. Shopping around keeps the price right.

Shrinkage and Damages

Shrinkage—better known by its more common names, shoplifting and stealing, is a major problem faced by every store owner. This cancer can be divided into two groups: dishonest customers and dishonest employees. In either case, it's stealing. The sad truth is that these thieves seldom, if ever, serve time for their dishonesty.

Again, shrinkage is another word for stealing, and stealing, whether by the amateur, the professional, or by your own help, is still stealing.

Protecting yourself from the professional shoplifter is a most difficult task (if not almost impossible). These thieves are often disguised as the most ordinary looking shoppers. A good shoplifter does not look like a thief. If we could just insist on the bad guys wearing black hats, it would make your job easier—but they don't.

The amateur shoplifter is sometimes easier to spot. I have heard it said that the largest *class* of shoplifters are suburban housewives. They usually have charge cards or the cash in their purses to pay for the items they have lifted. They either do it for kicks or with a mortgage, two or three kids, and owing for the refrigerator—there just isn't room in the family budget for what they steal.

There are two main reasons why these criminals can beat the rap:

1. Either the merchant does not want to be bothered by a court appearance as a witness, because it is too time-consuming, or he drops the charges if he gets his merchandise back. *In either case, the merchant is wrong.* The only way to stop this drain on your profits and the national economy is to prosecute. If there is no punishment, then the crime doesn't hurt anyone but you, and in the long run may hurt someone else.
2. In some cities, the court dockets are so full that by the time the thieves come to trial, the witnesses can't be found, resulting in loss of the evidence against them.

There are some shoplifters who suffer from mental illness; they simply can't help themselves. In many cases family and local police are aware of such problems and the families of these shoplifters make restitution to stores. In these special cases it is probably best to cooperate with the family (who can help keep the compulsive shoplifter out of your store) and not to prosecute.

Now let's look at your help. These are people with whom you will spend more *waking* hours per day than with your own spouse. You will eat lunch with them, tell them your troubles, listen to their troubles, and feel a certain kinship. It is hard and painful to imagine that these people could steal— but it happens.

Let me clarify this by saying that often they do not consider it stealing; they will try to justify their actions, e.g. "I ran my hose on your showcase, therefore you owe me a pair of hose." Justification? No!

A polygraph test is always a possibility—though an extreme one—and is reputed to be only about 90 percent accurate. It is used in the business community in varying degrees; some use it for new employees, others when shortages occurred, still others as a spot check—and others not at all. The laws vary from state to state on the use of the polygraph, so be sure to check beforehand with your attorney. The one thing you want to avoid is any hint of discrimination in the use of this test.

Damages are another story. There are several ways in which goods can become damaged:

1. They may be received that way from the manufacturer,
2. Damage may be due to the carelessness of customers or salespeople in the store, and
3. They may be returned by the customer after being worn. Let's take these one at a time in the light of a controlled expense.

1. If you receive goods from the manufacturer in damaged condition, you are well within your rights to return them. At this point you must check your invoice, since some vendors require a letter from you stating what the damage is, as well as how many pieces are involved, the style numbers, and a request for a "return authorization sticker." This sticker must be placed on the box containing the return so that your package will not be refused when it arrives at the vendor's factory.

This policy varies from vendor to vendor, so be sure to check their invoice for instructions. You will, of course, invoice the garment back (this is called a *charge-back*) and subtract this amount from any open invoices you owe this maker. In addition to the cost of the garment you are entitled to charge-back the freight, coming and going. Be sure you deduct what you are entitled to and no more.

Don't be picky! If the damage is so small that your alteration person can fix it with little effort, do not make a return —it's more trouble than it's worth. You never want to get the reputation of being a *returner*. A manufacturer can be a friend and is usually willing to help his customers by standing behind his product, but he will do little for someone who returns without truly legitimate reasons.

2. If merchandise is damaged by customers or salespeople, it should be repaired immediately upon discovery. Do not let the next customer find it, or your whole stock pales because of one bad garment. If the repair is minor and does not show (e.g. an open seam resewn), just put it back in stock. If, however, the repair shows, reduce the price to compensate for the damage and hang it on the sale rack. It is a good idea to make a tag that says "as is" and mark the sales slip accordingly so that there can be no question later and the customer knows exactly what he or she is getting. *Never try to fool the customer.* Aside from being dishonest, it's the worst way to do business.

3. Customer returns can become a very tricky area, and each case requires individual judgment. All stores have a return policy governing this particular customer's *right*, yet policies can be bent—and even broken—depending on the circumstance.

If you feel that the damage was the fault of the manufacturer (e.g., bad construction, poor piece goods, etc.), then satisfy your customer immediately and write your vendor for permission to return. Most vendors are anxious to please you and stand behind their product; they will either replace the garment or credit your account.

On the other hand, you look at the garment and it was obviously mistreated by the customer (e.g., washed in boiling water, faded by excessive perspiration, ripped, etc.) then you must make a determination based on your store policy. Some stores have a very liberal policy in this area—exchanges without questions—while others insist on the damages being the fault of the merchandise.

In addition to your store's policy, there is a hidden factor —how good a customer is it? A good customer can sometimes get away with murder, while you will do little or nothing for a chronic returner. Remember what was said in (1) above: chronic returners, both stores or retail customers—can expect little in the way of consideration or service.

We have now covered various expenses such as payroll, insurance, dues, advertising/display, subscriptions, telephones, utilities, office and store supplies, shrinkage, and damages. To these we might well add inflation—our seemingly constant companion in recent years, making prudent management of expense items a vital part of your business. As these costs keep rising, it becomes your job to find inventive ways to counteract this drain on your profits.

Your attention to what I like to call *creative management* separates you from a storekeeper and advances you toward what I described in Chapter 1 as a merchant.

Seven

Furniture and Fixtures

When there comes a time to sit...
it would be nice to have a chair!

Next to the purchasing of your inventory, furniture and fixtures will be your major expense when you open your new store. Even more important, it sets the image you wish to project. This is the area where you can spend as much as you wish, but if you are not careful, it is easy to overspend.

A basic rule when buying furniture and fixtures is: *you are in business to sell clothes—not racks!*

Even though your store must look good, do not get carried away with the idea that you must have polished teakwood when a less expensive wood will serve your purpose.

There is an alternative to opening a new store, and that is the purchase of an existing store. The purchasing of the furniture and fixtures is usually an area of disagreement between the seller and the buyer. You will feel that their furniture and fixtures are worth a fraction of what the seller thinks they're worth. You should be able to purchase them at something closer to your price, since the outgoing tenant is usually in no position to have them moved. There is absolutely nothing wrong with going into business by this route just as long as the fixtures are not damaged and do not look too old and beat up. Under these conditions, used fixtures will suffice and serve your needs. As I said, this is an alternative to buying all new. If you have the money to invest, you should seriously consider doing it *your* way. However, based on your type of operation, it is not always desirable to purchase new furniture.

Example: If you are opening a boutique operation, rummage through antique stores for period dressers, coat racks, mirrors, etc.—they project that certain image for this type of store. Once again, watch the prices. To achieve this dated look does not mean you have to buy "antique-antiques"; they just have to *look* old and cost less.

If you are working with a store designer, the cost depends on how tight a rein you hold on him (or her) and how much control you exercise: when starting with a store designer, have a clear understanding as to budget and image, and then make sure the designer stays with both. It is easy to get carried away and turn around one day and find that you have as much (or more) invested in the walls as in inventory.

Another pitfall to be aware of is the clash that can occur between you and the designer over the appearance you wish to achieve. If you never lose sight of the fact that the designer is there to guide you and that it is your money and your store, you can keep disagreements to a minimum. Do not ignore the designer's suggestions, since this is what you are paying for, but the final decision must always be yours.

Flexibility, Mobility, and Convenience

When laying out your store, remember that the floor racks are as important as your bins but for the most part serve a different purpose. Most stores use their walls for *regular*-priced merchandise while reserving the floor racks for *sale* or *reduced* goods. The floor should also be used to highlight special items or groups of related items (e.g. coordinated sportswear groups).

Wall bins should be flexible. By this I mean that the hang rod should be adjustable. Rods must be placed high to accommodate dresses and coats, while you should also be able to *double-deck* (two rods in the same bin, one over the other) to handle blouses, skirts, sweaters, men's suits or sport coats.

The primary reason for this versatility is that merchandise *must* be moved about the store. Do not permit the left wall to be dresses and stay that way forever. The season of the year is your major consideration when determining what hangs where. Example: in winter coats should have the prominent spot in the store; spring should be dresses; summer, sportswear and swimwear; fall can feature sweaters and pants. There are, of course, other items that fit the season and deserve the *starring role*. This you will learn as you get the feel of your store and the needs of your customers. Also, the examples given here vary with the section of the country. In Florida, winter may mean cruise sportswear and swimwear, while coats are relatively unimportant.

There are those merchants who would disagree with what I have said about moving merchandise around. They feel that they build customer identification with the various departments by leaving each in its own place. I truly believe that moving goods from one location to another in the stores makes customers think that they are seeing something new, especially since they may never have noticed the goods in its former spots.

Major stores maintain a complete display department for just this purpose. They not only move merchandise around —they move walls around. How many times have you walked

into a department store, walked straight to what you thought
was the blouse department, and found cosmetics? When you
asked a clerk, "Wasn't this the blouse department?" she
replied, "That was yesterday."

The key word when discussing the layout of your store is
convenience—convenience for your salespeople as well as
your customers. By departmentation and proper segregation
of the merchandise, you can create a traffic flow that can
mean added sales. This flow can be accomplished by keeping
the floor loose and not crowding your racks too closely
together; it has the additional advantage of giving the optimum view of the whole store while keeping to a minimum the
dead spots that are a shoplifter's delight.

Because of our modern modes of shopping, and in keeping
with controlled operating expenses, ready-to-wear stores
(and most other types of businesses) have taken their cue
from the supermarkets. As much as possible, all shopping today is *self-service*. This has greatly limited the types and
amount of merchandise kept under glass, i.e., in showcases.
Except for better jewelry and certain gift items, most goods
today are within easy reach of the customer. More and more
you will find items on open gondolas (display units) that were
formerly inside a case.

The reasons for this shift in merchandising policy are three-
fold: (1) it was discovered that customers who couldn't feel it
wouldn't buy it; (2) by having it open, "impulse buying" was
encouraged in most stores (think of what would happen to a
grocery store's volume if we all stuck to our shopping list and
never varied from it when we went shopping); (3) customers
who cannot wait on themselves require additional salespeople. This trend to self-service is as prevalent in smaller stores
as it is in department stores. The merchandising giants are all
moving in this direction in more and more departments.

Certain kinds of merchandise make natural neighbors in
the store and should be hung in close proximity to one

another. Example: hang blouses and tops near your skirts and pants. Put ties and dress shirts adjacent to the suit department for the add-on (additional) sale.

In reality, all stores are department stores no matter what size, and they can—and should—be departmentized. There are certain classes of merchandise that form natural departments unto themselves: dresses, sportswear, coats and suits, shoes, lingerie, accessories, men's suits and sport coats, slacks, sportshirts, dress shirts and accessories.

This is as good a time as any to speak of dressing rooms (sometimes called *fitting rooms*). Dressing rooms basically serve two purposes: (1) they are a place to try on a garment away from other people's eyes; this does not mean they are so secluded that it makes it difficult for your salespeople to service the customer or an easy place for shoplifters to ply their trade; and (2) they are a place to sell; this aspect of using the dressing room as a selling tool we will discuss at some length in our chapter on selling.

Are hangers fixtures? You bet they are! And important ones, too. Nothing looks worse in a store than to see a bin or rack with mixed hangers holding the same type of goods. Dresses should be on short-neck plastics—not some on wire, some on long-neck plastic, and some on wood. This mixture of hangers automatically detracts from the appearance of the merchandise and is very easily prevented. The exception to this rule may be where a coordinated sportswear group is on the same rack. In this case blouses, jackets, and vests (short-neck plastic) are hung with pants and skirts (short-clip hangers). Most stores use clear plastic, but if you opt for colored hangers, make sure that they are all the same color.

For many shoppers, a visit to stores is a day's outing. They will go from store to store and look at what's new. Sometimes they buy, more often they look. This, of course, is more true of a ladieswear operation than a men's store. Either way, *when a customer comes through your front door, consider him or her as a guest in your home.* Offer your guest a soft drink or coffee. They will feel more comfortable and wanted.

I have known stores that maintain a bar and offer cocktails. This I would not recommend for the small store; it is more usual with the better boutique.

Boutique is a French word meaning a *small specialty shop*, but with a slight difference—boutiques are usually more specialized in their selection of merchandise.)

Since boutique is a French word, Americans are prone to infer undeserved *class* and *couth*. It's normal. Do we not think French wine is better than California wine? French designers are better than American designers? French poodles are better than Boston Terriers? Well, California wine is great, American designers are among the finest in the world and poodles are German by origin. That should prove something.

What French boutiques were good at was making a profit. Using their penchant for *making a buck off the tourist*, the French were smart enough to put these shops where there was traffic—in hotels, airports, train stations, or any place where travelers were sure to visit.

We Americans, tourists, seeing these operations flourish, imported the idea as an alternative to department stores and large specialty stores (which were really small-apparel department stores) and proceeded to do our natural thing— we saturated the market.

How many *cutesie, adorable, pretty little shops* have you seen? Too many, right? Clever is one thing, cutesie is another. Make sure you know the difference.

A store is like a jigsaw puzzle: to complete the picture you must put all the pieces together to form the proper picture. The lighting, rugs, tiles, walls, paint, wallpaper, air conditioning, and heat are all selling aids. Let us examine these components individually.

Lighting

Most power companies employ experts on their staff to advise you as to the proper lighting design to reach the optimum light level at the most reasonable cost. *This service is done at no charge.* Different parts of your store require different types of lighting. Offices should be bright, selling areas more subdued, bins bright enough to be illuminated, yet soft enough so as not to fade the merchandise. Each of these areas will use different sizes and types of bulbs, fluorescent tubes, etc. Different levels of light throughout the store will tend to give the store an atmosphere and character that it is otherwise difficult to achieve.

We cannot discuss lighting without speaking of the windows. In Chapter 10 we will delve into windows and their importance, but here we will merely cover the lighting of those windows.

Since your windows are your most valuable selling aid, they should paint the best possible picture. I am a firm believer in *track lighting,* which offers you the versatility to highlight certain garments. With colored lights, used directly and indirectly, you can achieve variations of accent. As with most trade terms, *track lighting* means virtually what it says—spotlight bulbs are put in sockets mounted on a track attached to the ceiling or the window. They are completely adjustable by sliding along the track.

In addition, you might consider *floor spots.* These will give accent lighting from the bottom up rather than from the top down, and they are relatively inexpensive. They can be used in conjunction with track lighting.

Rugs and Tile

These two materials are known as *floor coverings;* they should not only beautify your store but should be serviceable. The term *floor covering* is not used here to be facetious, but rather to give the name used in leases when stating the landlord's responsibilities toward construction costs.

It is important that the colors chosen harmonize with the walls and ceiling. As with the lighting, the colors will add character and project a desired image. I always found it wise to mix carpeting and tiles throughout the store. Areas that contain better goods or the *heavy garments* (e.g., coats, suits, furs) should be carpeted. It adds a touch of richness. The front portion of the store can be tiled. In bad weather, the customers will track in water, mud, and snow, so if the front is tiled, it is easier to clean (and cheaper than replacing carpeting). It is better not to have too high a shag on the carpet, since this more easily catches a ladies' high heels and can cause an accident. Lawsuits you don't need! This is less of a problem in a men's store, but it should be seriously considered for the benefit of the women who accompany men.

Let's talk carpets: aside from the obvious—the right color and a low pile—consideration should be given to quality. Persian rugs are nice but not necessary. A good heavy-duty, cleanable carpet is what you need. As for color, *keep it neutral*. I usually worked with a deep beige or tan. The one time I worked closely with an interior designer I ended up with my prettiest store—but with a dark brown carpet. The effect was sensational, but so was the job of keeping it clean.

Walls, Paint, Pictures and Wallpaper

Walls are more than just something to keep the ceiling from falling down. With proper planning, walls create selling areas, hide storage and reserve stock, form dressing rooms, and provide privacy. Carefully selected colors of paint and wallpaper can make the store look larger, give an airy atmosphere, cut lighting bills (by the efficient diffusion of light), create a relaxed mood for the customers (which helps sell merchandise), and make for more happy and effective employees. Once again, this particular piece of the puzzle goes a long way toward building the image I have mentioned so often in these pages.

Once you have selected a *nonabusive* color scheme and shopped for the best and most reasonably priced painter, be sure that you don't overlook *washability*. Since it is bad public relations to forbid children in the store, be prepared for dirty hands, which cause dirty walls. The same holds true when choosing wallpaper.

Wallpaper, however, presents different considerations. In addition to color, be very careful when picking patterns. Remember, you are not decorating a kitchen or bedroom. What would be nice in your dining room could be *completely out of place on a store wall.* And it goes without saying (but I'll say it anyway) that the paint and wallpaper should be color-coordinated with the carpeting.

What goes on the walls is equally important. Pictures are nice if done in a subdued and inoffensive way. Here again you can overspend without really trying. A simple sconce from a department store can dress up a dressing room.

Do not buy prints of animals or seascapes unless you are a vet or a fish restaurateur. A way I found both effective and inexpensive was to go to a flea market and buy some very old *Cosmopolitan* or *Vogue* magazines. Clip interesting fashion pictures and frame them in *ready-made* frames.

There are a thousand easy ways to decorate walls, but keep one thing in mind: *don't overdo it.* Too little is always better than too much. Here again, remember that you are in business to sell your *products*, not pictures and screens.

Air Conditioning and Heat

Aside from the obvious—i.e., comfort—this is also considered a health factor; the filtered air and constant tempera-

ture will be credited with holding down the associated ill-
nesses, which in turn holds down absenteeism among your
employees.

But let us not lose sight of proper atmospheric conditions
as a selling tool. A layaway coat promotion in May, June, or
July will get better results in a cool store. A customer may be
reluctant to try a coat on when it is 90 degrees outside, so you
must create the atmosphere in the store. A cool store reminds
your customers of the cold weather to come while providing
them with the comfort to try on the garment and look in the
mirror. The reverse of this is true when selling cruisewear in
December.

Where your store is located will determine how you operate your air conditioning for maximum comfort and economy. In extremely hot climates, you may wish to let it run all
night and turn it off only on weekends. Since heat builds up
overnight, by turning off the a/c you could have a hot store
until noon before it cooled down. The morning heat load
could be both uncomfortable and uneconomical.

Heating and air conditioning can be controlled by the
proper setting of a thermostat. Let it do the work; do not help
it with the *off* and *on* switch.

Speaking of thermostats, we are immediately reminded of
the energy problems facing America today. The government
has requested settings for temperature controls to meet certain standards in public buildings.

Large structures such as office buildings, department
stores, and government offices do seem warm in summer and
cold in winter. This, of course, is almost the opposite of what
I said as to temperature being a selling tool. It would seem
that we as merchants are caught between a rack and a hard sell.

Your Office: Location and Furniture

The first area we should cover is the "cash stand." The cash
stand is also called "the office" and the "service desk." The

type of office furniture you select depends on whether your *office* is hidden or exposed. Obviously, the desk you choose should be nicer if your office is visible to the public. It goes without saying that any office, open or exposed, should be kept as small as possible. The reason for this is that you want to devote as much as possible of the of the square footage of your store to the selling area.

The convenience of your employees and customers should be your most serious consideration when determining location of an office within the store. A service-type office, often called *the desk* which is used for gift wrapping or paying on accounts, makes its location in the store very important.

If your store is oblong, the office should be placed in the rear of the building. The reason for this is to make the customer see as much of your stock as possible on each visit. If the store is nearly square, then place the desk as far back as possible, and to the left. Customers, depending on where the door is located, tend to move counterclockwise. By placing the desk back in the store, customers will be exposed to the maximum amount of merchandise even when they are just running in to pick up a package or only making a payment.

A final word regarding all furniture and fixtures: as much as possible, they should be both functional and expressive of your desired image.

Eight

Merchandising

Buy a little, sell a little—then reorder

Now that we have selected a location, signed a lease with the landlord, arranged for the financing, arrived at a control of expenses, purchased our furniture and fixtures, we have fought all the preliminary bouts. Now comes the main event —*buying the merchandise*.

This immediately raises two questions: (1) what to buy? and (2) how much to buy? The answer to *what* is based on the type of store you intend to operate. By type of store I do not mean just a small store selling clothes. Within the category of small clothing stores we find a vast variety of types.

There are stores specializing in jeans, juniors, men's, half-sizes, and couture—plus many others doing business in stores, old houses, fair stalls, flea markets, or almost any building that can hold a rack of clothes. Each in its own way must be stocked with wares geared to the customer who will frequent that type of establishment. This buying of the right goods for a particular business is called *merchandising*.

The answer to *how much* is your open-to-buy or OTB.

Open-to-buy (OTB) is a trade term used to describe the number of dollars to be spent, or units to be bought, for any given period of time in each department. When Moses came down from the mountain God had given his OTB for the children of Israel. It was the OTB for a better life on earth and an OTB for getting into Heaven. Another word for OTB is *plan*.

Merchandise does not appear on your racks by magic. Much time, effort, worry, stress, soul-searching, and knowledge go into selecting and buying the proper goods in the proper quantities. You can't eat like an elephant and be built like a bird. Your purchase must be in direct relationship to your sales.

Merchandising is another name for management—managing the ebb and flow of inventory into your store. Remember these two old clichés:

1. "Plan your work and work your plan."
2. "You can't do business from an empty wagon."

Trite but pertinent!

Too little inventory gives customers the impression that you have a limited selection. Since the customers are always right, they are doubly right in this case. Too much inventory can cause markdowns, which, if allowed to get out of hand, can put you out of business.

Too many small business people never give a thought to how much inventory they have piling up. *Merchandise must be thought of as money*: money to pay the help, money to pay the bills, money to put the kids through college. Granted, money just "ain't what it used to be"—but until we go back to the barter system it's the only game in town.

Controlling this inventory is one of the things that separate the shopkeeper from the merchant. I know I pointed out this difference in terms before, but a truism bears repeating.

Merchandising can be likened to a teeter-totter. Your store

is on one end of the board selling and your vendors are on the other end shipping. Your job is to balance this game and keep it on an even keel.

I touched lightly before, and heavier later, on markdowns as an evil of being caught in an overbought condition. There are other pains you can suffer by using "too big a pencil for writing orders."

Consider the tied-up capital that prevents you from buying *hot items* when all of your money is tied up in *dead* stock. Think of the poor merchant who was riding the crest of unbelievable sales in Hoola Hoops some years ago. It looked like a craze that would go on forever, so what did he do? He bought a six-month's supply (based on sales and expected sales) and warehoused them. We all know what came next. The bottom of the Hoola Hoop market fell out. If you ask today's young people what a Hoola Hoop is, they can't tell you.

This is even a greater possibility when we discuss the ready-to-wear industry. A dress that is sensational today is dead tomorrow. A man's polyester leisure suit went from hot to cold in mid-season. If you will recall Chapter 1: Management—an Art or a Science?: well, in running your inventory it's both! The art of inventory control is to bring as much science into it as possible. The *science* or the *art* is called your *open-to-buy* or OTB.

In an established store, your OTB is based on the previous year's sales for the period in question. The formula is rather simple and requires basic arithmetic. We will cover this later under Reorders, below; but for now let's think in terms of opening a new store without any of last year's figures to guide you.

We have established that inventory purchases are in direct relationship to sales, and, with no previous sales figures, we have only two things to guide us: *space* and *estimated sales*. The first is an absolute and the second is an estimate.

Space and Sales Methods
Your "Open-To-Buy" (OTB)

Space

For openers, let us examine how an *OTB* is calculated based on space. Assuming that your store was built from blueprints, you will have before you a store layout. By knowing the size and number of bins, shelves, and racks that you will have, we can estimate the amount of goods it will take to stock the store. Let us assume that you intend to devote six bins to dresses. We know that a bin holds approximately 50 garments; therefore, you must have 300 dresses to fill the bins. Different items will either increase or decrease the capacity of the bins based on the bulkiness of the goods.

By applying the same formula to every department, you can come up with a starting OTB. This is not foolproof, just a rule of thumb. Remember, *your store should never look empty*. To prevent this, some merchants stay in a constant overbought condition. Either condition—overbought or underbought—is not good. As we have said, your goal should be to strike a proper balance; however, the longer you are in business, the harder this task may seem.

The most important stock you will ever buy will be your opening inventory. It is at this point that your reputation is established. Since word-of-mouth advertising is vital to your success (this will be covered more fully in a later chapter devoted to advertising), you do not want to disappoint those first shoppers. If you are ever to be overstocked, let it be now. Why? First, because you do not want to make a bad impression; second, you don't really know how much business you can do, and you want to miss as few sales as possible.

Estimated Sales

When working an OTB on the space method, you must use estimated sales figures in conjunction with it to arrive at the final numbers. Let me explain how and why this becomes necessary: after using the blueprint to figure the amount of hang-rod space that must be filled, you now allow for the immediate *rush* of business that will deplete your stock. These sales, which will remove goods from your stock, must be replaced—otherwise, you are back to that empty look again. Therefore, you will estimate the sales for at least the first 60 days. At the time when you place your initial orders for the goods that you must have for the opening, you will place *additional* orders to come in at *staggered* times to keep the stock filled in. What you are doing, in reality, is placing your reorders before you sell the goods. This is tricky, and you will lean (to a degree) on your sales reps and manufacturers.

To do all this (using estimated sales), you must research what businesses of your size and in your locality do on an average, month to month. There are several places to obtain this type of information: The Small Business Administration, university economic research departments, chambers of commerce, local and state industrial commissions, and trade associations.

Once you have these average figures, compare the first 90 days of estimated volume to the amount of goods it takes to fill the racks. *You should have your first 90 days' sales as your opening inventory.* Remember, not all of your original purchases will arrive before you open the front doors, so this will automatically give you a flow for the first 30 days. Recall that you will have placed additional orders in the beginning to ensure an ample stock during your initial selling period; these orders can be adjusted based on how you are meeting your estimated sales.

This seems like the logical time to discuss markup, markdowns, and reorders:

Markup

Markup is the term applied to that portion of the selling price over and above your wholesale cost. The formula for arriving at the percentage of markup on the retail method is: *divide the selling (retail) price into the difference between the retail price and the wholesale cost.* For example: wholesale cost is $5, retail (or selling) price is $10, the difference is $5. When you divide the retail ($10) into the difference ($5) it equals 50 percent.

Retail	$ 10		
			.50%
Cost	$ 5	10.00	5.0000
			5.000
Difference	$ 5		0

The tendency here is to think of this as 100 percent markup. It *is* 100 percent of the cost, but it is only a 50 percent markup at retail.

In today's inflated market, a 50 percent markup is a bare survival figure. You cannot get rich on this markup when the cost of everything is as high as it is and with little sign of going down. In the 1950s, a 40 percent markup was the going figure, but today you would go broke on 40 percent.

Before every discounter and budget store yells "Foul," let me be quick to point out that some stores can, and do, operate on less than a 50 percent markup. However, there is a

METHOD OF OBTAINING FIXED MARKUP PERCENTAGE
TO FIND MINIMUM REQUIRED SELLING PRICE

For 25% Markup	Divide cost by 3 and add this amount to cost.
	Example: Cost $120.00 divided by 3 equals $40.00
	$120.00 plus $40.00 equals $160.00
	$160.00 is the retail selling price
	at 25% markup.

For 33⅓% Markup — Divide cost by 2 and add this amount to cost.
Example: Cost $120.00 divided by 2 equals $60.00
$120.00 plus $60.00 equals $180.00
$180.00 is the retail selling price
at 33⅓% markup.

For 40% Markup — Divide cost by 3. Multiply this figure by 5.
Example: Cost $120.00 divided by 3 equals $40.00
$ 40.00 multiplied by 5 equals $200.00
$200.00 is the retail selling price
at 40% markup.

For 45% Markup — Divide cost by 11. Multiply this amount by 20.
Example: Cost $120.00 divided by 11 equals $10.91
$10.91 multiplied by 20 equals $218.20
$218.20 is the retail selling price
at 45% markup.

For 50% Markup — Multiply cost by 2.

---

catch: The stores that can operate on a substandard markup offer little if any *services*. Remember, each time you offer the customer any service (e.g., charge accounts, gift wrapping, layaways), it adds to your cost of operation and therefore must be compensated in the markup that you apply to your merchandise.

When I say, "You would go broke on 40 percent, I am

assuming you will be running a legitimate full-service specialty store. If this is the case, then the assumption is correct.

As a rule, most stores use one of two formulas for applying
a retail price to the cost. If a garment costs $14.75, they multi-
ply the *first two* numbers by 2 for a $28 retail, while other
stores add .25, making the cost $15, and then multiply by 2
for a $30 retail. Nothing less than the above will produce a
profit.

Most chains, department stores, and specialty stores use
this method because all of their thinking is at the retail (e.g.,
sales, markdowns, inventory,), as opposed to using the
wholesale cost price to compute this information.

The table on page 91 will show you a fast method of
calculating the exact amount in dollars and cents that you
must get at retail to realize the markup percentages as given.
(Since markup is a matter of store policy, which only you can
set, this chart is merely for guidance.)

Markdowns

Markdowns are the bugaboo of every merchant. They are
a direct charge to profits and an automatic decrease to your
maintained markup.

Markdowns can result from a number of factors. Over-
stocking, poor style selections, change of season, and change
of fashion. Will Shakespeare once said, as if to prove this
statement, "I see that fashion wears out more apparel than
the man." With the exception of changing fashions, any of
the other factors are controlled, *to a degree*, by the proper
working of your own *OTB*. A change in style can be somewhat controlled by keeping yourself properly informed by
reading the fashion forecasts in your trade publications,
shopping the market intelligently, and staying in constant
contact with your customers. The changes in style to which I

refer are *drastic* changes, not the normal changes that occur each season.

This does not include those markdowns that result from damages and customer returns. These are too small to be counted (or at least should be), as we have already observed.

Since *markdowns are a direct charge to profits*, we must look for ways to offset this drain on markup as much as possible. Aside from astute buying and controlled OTB, one of the best methods is the purchase of *off-priced* (OP) goods. To illustrate the purchasing of OP goods, let me give you the following example: at the end of the season, which always occurs earlier at the manufacturing level than in the store, the factory takes its markdowns. You, as a merchant, may be offered an opportunity to purchase this merchandise at a reduced price. *Thus by leaving yourself open to buy additional goods (based on estimated sales) at a lower price, you can realize a higher markup.* When averaged against your markdowns, this gives you an overall markup that you can live with.

For example: A garment that costs $19.75 and that retails for $40 (a 50.6 percent markup) can now be purchased off-price for $11.75. If, based on previous selling records of this *very same style*, or based on *similar goods* that have sold well in your store, you decide to purchase this merchandise, you will put it into stock at $40, giving you a 70.6 percent markup. This applies only to garments that are not already reduced in your store. If you have similar goods already reduced (let's say to $29, or a 33.9 percent markup based on the $19.75 cost), you can average the two lots together and have a 54.9 percent markup overall. If you mark it $40, your selling time on the off-price merchandise is limited (remember that you bought it near the end of the season), so you will be marking it down soon. When it is finally reduced to $29.90, you have an average markup of 47.3 percent. This is the markup I said you can live with.

If all this sounds confusing—it shouldn't! The formula is simple and unchanged from the one given previously! *Retail minus cost, the difference divided by retail.* Let us apply this formula to the above example:

2 Garments @ $29.90		= $59.80
1 Cost	$19.75	
1 Cost	$11.75	
Total Cost	$31.50	− $31.50
Difference		$28.30

Divide $59.80 into $28.30 for a 47.3 percent markup. Now wasn't that simple?

Cliche #9463: *Your first markdown is your cheapest.* Think of this theory as a formula when applied to your goods. Reduce a garment 20 percent and it does not sell. Reduce it to ⅓ off and it still does not sell. You will finally have to reduce it to ½ off because it's getting too old—and now it sells! You would have been better off reducing it to 25 percent immediately and moving it out while it was still close to the customer's time of need. In so doing, you would have saved yourself 17 to 25 percent in markdowns.

To be sure, this is a *theory*. There are times when even ½ price will not move the garment from your stock. In the terminology of the trade, this is a *"dog."* It is now that you must find the price that someone is willing to pay. Some storekeepers (note I did not say *merchants*) worry about the original cost when taking markdowns. *Never* think of what a garment cost at wholesale when taking markdowns—only think of what it will take to sell. If it is a "dog," there is no price too cheap. It is always better to turn the garment into some cash (no matter how little) with which to purchase new and (hopefully) saleable goods. Recalling the earlier discussion of the chemise dress, I sold dresses that cost $29.75 for $5.99 because they were *dogs*; if I had considered the cost of those dresses, they would be almost 30 years old, and I would still own them.

Reorders

Reorders are the lifeblood of any business. When you reorder, it means that you have sold the merchandise and that you need more based on the demand of your customers. If you buy ten pieces of a style and sell all ten—that's good. If you buy ten pieces of a style and through reorders end up selling 60 to 100 pieces—**that's sensational!** As a merchant, this is what you are constantly looking for—but, more importantly, this is what you must have!

There is a pitfall to reordering! *Know when to stop!* This is as important as knowing when to start. One of the primary offenders in creating markdowns is having too much inventory at the change of season. Reorders can cause this condition. It is better to lose the last two or three sales than mark down the last 15 or 20 pieces left in stock from one reorder too many. That last reorder can also keep you from taking advantage of off-price offers, and your markup is thereby affected.

No one can really teach you this. What we are actually discussing here is the difference between a storekeeper and a merchant—and it *hopefully* will come to you with experience.

OTB Based on Previous Year's Sales

We discussed earlier how to work an *OTB* using space as your guide. If you have the previous year's figures, it becomes more of a science. This we can do mathematically. Here again the formula is simple and there is no cause for panic. We will use a four-time turn. A "turn" is that specific length of time it would take to sell your inventory in any given department (e.g., dresses, sportswear) if you received no additional merchandise. Example: your inventory at the end of a month was $900. Your sales for the next three months were $300 per month. Theoretically in three months you would have no inventory. By taking your selling time and dividing it into 12 (the number of months in a year), you get 4, therefore three months' selling equals a four-time turn. Four months' sales equals a three-time turn; two months' sales equals a six-time turn, etc..

For the sake of this example, let us use the three-month OTB period of January through March for our calculations.

1. Estimate sales for each department by the month, using last year's figures as your guide.
2. Add the estimated sales for the three months of February, March, and April together (never use the month whose ending inventory you are trying to determine—in this instance, January). The total of these three months will give you the ending inventory figure for January 31st.
3. Compare ending and beginning inventories for January. Beginning inventory for January would be December 31st. Taking the difference and adding (or subtracting if ending is smaller than beginning) to January estimated sales will give you January's OTB. This process is repeated for each month. To get February's OTB, you will use January 31st as the beginning inventory and the total estimated sales for March, April, and May as your ending figure. The following will illustrate this formula:

Beginning Inventory	Estimated Sales				Ending Inventory	Jan. OTB
	Jan.	Feb.	Mar.	Apr.		
$1000	$300	$200	$400	$300	$900	$200

+ 100
OR
MIN. 200

1000 - 900 = 100

As we said, we want three months' selling to equal ending inventory. Since we do not count the month we are working (January sales), we take February, March and April to arrive at the $900. figure. Our ending inventory is $100 less than our beginning inventory so we want to reduce our OTB by that amount. However, we have $300 to do in sales for January. Therefore, we subtract the reduction in inventory ($100) from the estimated sales ($300) and that leaves us an OTB of $200 for the month of January. If the ending inventory was greater than the beginning inventory, we would add the difference to the expected sales for January to reach the OTB.

To determine February's OTB we use the same formula, but January's ending inventory becomes our beginning inventory, and we add together March, April, and May's expected sales to reach February's ending inventory. And so on . . . and so on . . . and so on! This of course is all based on a four-time turn.

What I have shown you is done for each department individually (e.g. misses' dresses, junior dresses, sportswear). Your CPA may have another method, but *be careful*, since working OTB's may be out of your accountant's area of expertise. Remember, the most important part of this formula is the estimating of sales for each month, since all figures depend on the *expected* sales figures. There are many factors to consider when estimating sales. What was the weather last year during the period being worked? Was there a particularly hot item last year that distorted last year's sales figures? Are you running ahead or behind in that department this year? In short, you must think—and treat your OTB as the living, breathing thing it is.

It is important always to be aware that your own OTB is worked well in advance and that business conditions are constantly changing, so that your OTB may need revision. If your sales are running well ahead of estimate, then you will want

Check Out Book Page

DEPT. *JR. DRESSES*   SEASON *SUMMER*

Name *ABC FROCKS*   (214)
                                                    No. *321-4685*

Address *200 PACIFIC ST.*   Terms *8/10 EOM*

       DALLAS, TX. 75245

		REORDERS				RECEIVED			
		DATE	QUAN.	DATE	QUAN.	DATE	QUAN.	DATE	QUAN.
STYLE	1620	4/29/	10						
COST	14.75								
RETAIL	30.00								
DESCRIPTION	SLVLESS , A-LINE SUNBACK PRINT								

	DATE	QUAN.	COLOR	5	7	9	11	13				
	4/18	5	BLUE	/		4/24		4/23				
			PINK		4/21	/						

to adjust your OTB upward for that period. Conversely, a slowdown in sales will require a review of your "outstanding paper" (order copies) with an eye to reevaluating. To put it in the simplest way possible: live with your own OTB.

Your Check-Out Book (Inventory Control)

In connection with your *OTB*, one of the most important records you will keep is your *"check-out" book*. There are probably as many different ways to keep this particular record as there are merchants. A definition of a *check-out book* is simply a day-to-day record of merchandise received and sold by vendor, style number, description, cost, retail, color and size.

This is not a difficult record book to create. A page is set up in a loose-leaf notebook with the vendor's name at the top of the page. You record one or more styles per page with a system for marking off sales. The accompanying illustration shows a sheet that I used in my stores. Yours can be a variation of mine, or you have my permission to copy it exactly.

It is with this check-out book that you will reorder good styles and mark down poor selling styles. Both areas are important to the proper management of your business. If a manufacturer wants to know how his line is performing in your store, it is vital that you have this information to show him. You create this record by having a price ticket on the garment with a portion that can be detached (stub) at the time of sale. This *stub* should then be posted to the check-out book the next day.

Your check-out book (or inventory control) can serve many purposes other than those mentioned above. If this book is maintained properly, it becomes a merchandising tool whereby you can determine overbought and—equally important—underbought conditions before they can do real damage.

Check-out records are a must when shopping for off-price goods. As we noted before, it is important to know what you sold of an article before buying more, even at a reduced price. Your records will also tell you (by description) what type of goods you have done well with, so that even if you are not buying exactly the same item, you can at least get close.

Your check-out book should provide you with all the information you need for filling in (replacing goods sold) on basic items (e.g., hose, socks, white shirts); it should tell whether you are reordering hot items soon enough and in enough depth; which vendors are profitable and which are causing the greatest number of markdowns; whether you have inadvertently bought the same item, or type of items, from different manufacturers (and if so, whose is selling best); and whether your sizes and colors in a given department are balanced in accordance with their sales.

Four Key Questions

A primary rule to remember at this time is that you are a specialty store. What this means in its truest sense is that you can't be all things to all people. Even Macy's can't do this.

There is a story told that many years ago Marshall Field, the merchandising giant of Chicago, ran an ad stating that it would pay $100 to any customer who could walk into the store and request an item that they did not have in stock. An old Jewish man came in and asked for a *Mezuzah* (a small religious article fixed to a doorpost or worn on the person), and they did not have it. He walked out with $100. True or not, this story underscores the point that no matter how big you are, you can't carry everything.

Every store must fill a niche in the business community where it is located. Before you purchase your first piece of goods, you must answer certain key questions.

1. What price lines will I concentrate on? Budget, moderate, or better
2. What departments can I live without?
3. What image should my store project?
4. Whom do I want for customers?

Now, let us look at and examine all of the above, one at a time.

Price Lines

The words *budget*, *moderate*, and *better* mean different things to different people. There are, however, standard definitions accepted within the industry—although with inflation, the standards vary as the years go by. The words *budget*, *moderate*, or *better* are used to describe general price ranges. As an example: in the dress department, a *budget* dress has no bottom price and can sell for as much as $55; *moderate*-price dresses will sell for $60 to $140; and *better* dresses sell from $150 up. Major stores today have created a new category called *"bridge."* This comes between moderate and better and sells for $80 to $150.

To illustrate this point let me tell you a story that happened to me many years ago.

I still had my group of stores when a friend of mine (a salesman) called me and said his wife had two girlfriends who wished to open a store. Money was no problem and the reason for the store was to relieve boredom and give the women something to do other than play golf and bridge. I met with them and the first question I asked was, "What price lines do you intend to carry? Budget, moderate, or better?" They thought for a few minutes and said, "Moderate!" To assure that we were not comparing apples to oranges, I asked, "What do you consider a moderate-price dress?" The answer was, "About $150 must be moderate."

The above story is not as ridiculous as it may sound at first. In these women's circle of friends, the statement had merit and was probably true. However, in the real world, somewhere between $40 and $60 was moderate at that time. Postscript: the two women were fast and willing learners. They opened their store and carried moderate-to-better merchandise, and today they are very successful.

There is no magic to selling fashion, or any other product for that matter. Give your customers what they want, when they want it, and at a price they can afford, and you have just become a success!

What Departments Can I Live Without?

Here we come back to the word *specialty* when describing the store. Will my main thrust be sportswear or dresses? Will I be known as a good coat store? Should I have a shoe department? Are all areas of lingerie necessary?

All of these questions can be answered by shopping your competition and seeing what is lacking in their inventory. However, you must also consider that there may be a reason for them not stocking the items you see missing. Your choice of departments will also be governed, to some extent, by your own financial condition. Always keep in mind that you have to pay for everything you buy and that in most cases you are paying for it before you sell it.

You can always add departments, but closing departments can be injurious to your image. Every time you offer a customer a new department it carries the connotation of growth. The reverse is true when you discontinue a department. But do not let this theory be too rigid. If you are losing money in a department, it is better to stop carrying the item, but try to replace it with something new.

What Image Should My Store Project

This is the trickiest question of all to answer. Image is more than price lines. It includes service, appearance of the help, windows, advertising, and the like. If you project a *high* fashion image, you run the risk of scaring off potential customers because they may think that you are too expensive. If you project too moderate an image, you may find it difficult to sell your better goods. If your stock is completely *better*, then your image should tell that to all who come in. But if you are a moderate-price operation and wish to be a good $60-to-$80 dress store or want to sell men's suits at $125, then you had better also stock goods at a higher price level. You need this *umbrella* to help move the goods that you really want to sell.

Whom Do I Want for Customers?

At this point, let us talk age, sizes, and look.

Do not confuse age and size. In this modern world of fashion, a 50-year-old mother will interchange wardrobes with her 18-year-old daughter. After all, a pair of jeans is a pair of jeans. An easy place to fall into the age trap is in juniors. Years ago, the word junior meant *only* young. *Today, junior is a size, not only an age!* If a woman is short-waisted, she will wear a size 9, not a size 10. Since odd-numbered sizes are referred to as *juniors*, age is not the consideration—only the proper fit of the garment.

Even though what I have said with regard to juniors is true, there are still those who associate the word *junior* with "young." When we say "the junior market," we are basically speaking of lines that project a young image and that are geared for that customer. But when you take into consideration what I said about the mother and her 18-year-old daughter, this whole discussion becomes academic.

Here is where *look* enters the picture. It is true that there are some styles that lend themselves to a more mature woman, while there are others that are simply *too young*. There are other looks that were designed for a specific category of customer, such as the *career woman*. However, in every case you will see customers buying garments that don't fit the image.

Stand on a busy corner and become a people-watcher. If you are downtown in a large city, the men may all be in pin-striped vested suits, while the women are all in dresses. Here again, age is not a factor. Even though they think they are dressing to their individual taste, the *feeling* you get will be one of uniformity. Stand in a suburban shopping center and the look changes drastically to a more casual feeling. Play this whole scene in a small town and you get a different feeling again.

This feeling for the area surrounding your store is interpreted into image for your store. You will cater to the customer walking past your front door to a great extent, and the need your store must fill in the community will complete your merchandising plan.

Nine

Sales Reps and Manufacturers

When marching to a different "drummer"...
make sure you get deliveries on time.

Sales representatives: Who are they? What are they? Why are they...and: can I live without them?

All of these are legitimate questions, and I will attempt to answer them as objectively as possible after 25 years of exposure to the best and the worst in the business.

Who are they? A good sales rep is your eyes and ears to the industry, your guide through the mazes of indecision, the caverns of confusion, the heights of good lines and the depths of poor lines. A good sales rep can be the doctor who cures the disease of overconfidence, the rash of impetuousness, the fever of despair, and the cramps that come with being overbought. A good rep is a coach who calls plays, sends in substitutes, trades bad players, and finds the ones that can go all the way.

In short, a good sales-rep is your teacher and friend. A bad sales rep is an enemy to your profits and one to be feared. Your job: sort them out! Now that you know your job—sorting them out—let us look at the procedure of doing just that.

The old cliché of not being able to judge a book by its cover holds particularly true when discussing sales reps. Some are the strong silent types (although this species is somewhat rare), some are loud, some are funny (these usually are rejects from show biz), some *seem* sincere, some seem insincere, some you like immediately, while some you may be tempted to dislike just as fast, some try to overpower you, while others use a *softsell*. If all this sounds confusing—it is!

Sales reps, although in a somewhat different class, are pretty much like normal, everyday human beings. They each have their good points—and sometimes their bad. In my many years as a buyer, I have been fooled in both directions. Some whom I thought were honest, sincere people interested in my wellbeing turned out to be just the opposite. There were others who were a pleasant surprise and later became close friends.

My personal instincts always rebelled against any fast-talking, overpowering type who came on like a sideshow barker. If someone tried to impress me with his *vast* knowledge, at the expense of my own intelligence, it always made me leery. I expected my sales reps to guide me as honestly as possible and to sell their own product on its merit alone, without using the negative approach of defaming their competition. If they couldn't sell me their line on its merits alone, I usually passed.

All in all, judging the people calling on you will be one of the hardest things you have to do as a buyer, and much as I hate to say this, it mostly comes with experience.

What are they? Good sales reps are people who have learned their trade and because of their experience can be classified as experts on their line and, in some rare cases, as experts on a specific type of merchandise. Notice that I said *on their line*.

They should know their line just by the fact that they talk to enough buyers and make their decisions based on a consensus of their customers' opinions and purchases.

Good sales reps try their best to guide you down the right path. Poor sales reps are interested only in the order they are writing at the moment and care little for your welfare. Good sales reps want you to do well with their goods so that a meaningful relationship will result in future business. Like your reorders, repeat customers are their lifeblood.

Why are they? Why they exist is obvious. You as a buyer/ storeowner have neither the time nor the money to constantly be in the major markets (Dallas, L.A., or New York) to keep abreast of the style changes, to purchase merchandise, and generally to keep attuned to matters important to the operation of your business.

Good sales reps serve all of the above functions. They bring the market to you when you cannot go to it, while serving as your guide when time permits you to travel. They push you in the right direction, and through their knowledge they attempt to keep you from falling into pits on the road to profits. And they can, at times, assist when mistakes occur by curing the problem through many devices at their disposal.

Can I live without them? Good sales reps, *no!* Poor sales reps, *yes!* To sum it all up briefly, a good sales rep is an asset, while a poor sales rep does little or nothing to help you.

Sales reps are a funny lot. If you admit your shortcomings and ask for their help and guidance, they will break their backs for you. However, try to fool them and they resent the insult to their intelligence.

A Matter of Common Courtesy

Time to a sales rep, like to yourself, is money. Just as you should not waste your time, do not waste his time. It is easy, as a buyer or store-owner, to be lulled into a feeling of self-importance and a feeling of superiority to those selling you. This, too, can be injurious to the health of your business.

In the operation of my stores, I insisted that my buyers always greet and talk to any sales reps calling on them. It is rare that any line presented will be totally without value. True, you may not be *open-to-buy* or you may already have purchased elsewhere what they want to show you—but that is no excuse to let them *cool their heels* waiting to see you, only to be sloughed off. Show them the courtesy of either looking at their line or making a later appointment that is convenient to you both.

Some buyers are guilty of a bad attitude toward sales reps, and when they need help from them, it is not forthcoming. My father, who was not only a good merchant but a fine gentleman, taught me early in my career, "Always treat a salesman with respect because there may come the day when you need him more than he needs you." He proved this point during World War II when clothing went on allotments and many stores couldn't get goods. Dad's problem was not getting overbought.

Do not judge a sales rep solely on appearance. It is sometimes easy to look at a rep and decide that you do not like the way he dresses or parts his hair, or the fact that he wears a beard. Listen to what he has to say, and if he is knowledgeable, act on his advice. On the other hand, if he is dressed completely out-of-style, this could affect any credence in what he has to say.

Manufacturers

Manufacturers—aside from the most basic definition of "those who manufacture and who are the employers of the sales reps", can be described in much the same manner as the sales rep. In addition, they can assist you far beyond the scope and authority of their sales reps, and in that respect, they gain tremendous importance to you as a store owner.

Factory owners, with their highly technical staff, are responsible for the styling, making, and shipping of the merchandise that will, in the long run, help to make or break your store. It is in their province to create and deliver to you fashions that will sell. But it is *your* decision as to what lines you will buy. If you feel that a given manufacturer has not met the above conditions, then don't buy his line!

The manufacturing process covers a multitude of decision-making areas. It begins, as I said, with the creation of style. A great deal of time and effort is spent by manufacturers, their design staffs, and research teams in *putting together a line* that they feel will fit the needs of the stores they service. Just as your store must fill a particular niche in your area, so every manufacturer must fill a niche in the industry. Not every line is right for every store. A good manufacturer picks his outlets for both maximum exposure and sales.

Each manufacturer must fill that niche in the industry we keep talking about. Except for the largest, most manufacturers do not produce a line suitable to the entire country. Weight, color, and styling are prime factors and are usually geared to the general region in which the manufacturer is located. Putting his goods into the *wrong* stores can hurt him more than the few sales he will realize.

Once the team at the factory has reached its decisions, fabrics are selected and sample garments are made. It is at this point that manufacturers, along with their production people, review the sample garments to determine fit and saleability. Since each firm, as I said, must fill its niche in a store, it becomes important that its garments' cost price fit the category of the people they hope to sell.

When all of the above is established, duplicate yardage is ordered from the mills. Additional samples are made for the merchandising arm of their organization to take into their territories. Each salesperson thus has one sample of every garment to be made for the coming season. Based on selling reports, production estimates are made, additional material is ordered from the mills, and the actual sewing operations begin. Manufacturers have two primary responsibilities remaining to them at this point: delivery and quality control.

Delivery Date

All of the above is meaningless if the merchandise does not arrive in your store on time and as per the sample shown you at the time of purchase. At the time you write your order, there is a space marked *delivery date*. It is of the utmost importance that you fill this in properly. No order is completed without a date in this section. If you were to look at order copies written by various buyers you would see a variety of notations (e.g. A/R, 1/15 comp, blank, 2 weeks). Because of what I have already said, obviously not all of the notations shown could be correct. *A/R*, which means "*as ready*," gives you absolutely no control over your order. *Blank* is wrong for every reason that you can think of, while a definite time specified, such as *2 weeks* or *1/15 complete* is right. If you put down *A/R 1/15 comp*, what you are telling the manufacturer is that they may ship you anytime after receipt of order, but no later than January 15th. *Two weeks* means just what it says: ship now, because you have only two weeks to get the merchandise to me. In reality, what you are doing is setting forth a pre-agreed time for the manufacturer to deliver the merchandise. This is not an arbitrary date that you write, but *it is one agreed upon with the sales rep at the time of purchase.*

I have tried to be quite emphatic on this matter of delivery for a specific reason. For you to control your purchases, you must know at all times how much you have in inventory, your expected sales, and how much you will be receiving during any given period of time. Without definite delivery dates, you cannot know the latter. This protection works for both you and the manufacturer. You, as the retailer, have the right to cancel late shipments and thereby control your flow of goods, while the manufacturer is within his legal rights to ship the goods before completion date. Manufacturers who accept an early cancellation are doing so out of the goodness of their hearts and a sense of both your and their own well-being: for you, to help you out of an overbought condition; for them, so that they can come back and sell you again.

Quality Control

The second area of manufacturers' responsibility is quality control of their product. What you see is that you *should* get! A manufacturer must ship you as per sample shown at the time of purchase. If for any reason the merchandise you receive is not exactly *as ordered*, you are within your legal rights to return it to the maker based on the stipulations that appear on your order copy. Always keep in mind that your order copy is a *contract* between you and the manufacturer and that you both must adhere to its conditions.

Let me tell you a story from my days as a young buyer. We were doing business with one of the largest makers of dresses in the country. This firm would invariably substitute either sizes or colors, and sometimes even piece goods—never less than two out of these three. Finally I walked into their show-room (in New York) with a scissors, and after I wrote the line, I started to cut a small piece of goods from the inside of the hem and attach it to my order copy. As I was doing this, the owner happened by and asked me just what I thought I was doing. I told him that the *only* way I could be sure that what I received was what I bought was to have a sample. My shipments were better after that.

Let me say here that the vast majority of manufacturers are honest businessmen who have your welfare at heart. As with any large group, you may find *"bad apples,"* but he is the exception.

Buying and Dealing

When my stores were in full bloom, I employed up to six buyers. A different buyer was responsible for individual departments. In running a small store, you, or perhaps you and an assistant, will be responsible for all departments. With so many lines being offered, it can be confusing as to where to buy and from whom.

One way to alleviate some of this confusion is through the use of a *resident buying office*. When my firm operated three stores we hired a New York resident office. As our organization grew, we added the services of a Los Angeles office. We never had a Dallas resident office, since this was our home base.

A resident buying office is a firm located in a major apparel production center (e.g., Dallas, Los Angeles, New York) that acts as a purchasing agent and source of information for retail store clients.

Resident buying offices are basically two types, (1) a paid office and (2) a commission office.

Paid Office and Commission Office

A *paid office* is one where you pay a flat fee for their services. This fee is usually based on your store's volume. A *commission office* collects nothing from *you* but rather is paid a commission from the *manufacturer* on orders placed with them for you by the office.

On the face of it, it would seem that a *paid office* would have a hard time finding clients since a *commission office* is free. The truth of the matter is that paid offices are the stronger.

In either case, your choice of an office is very important, and so they should be checked out thoroughly. This is done by interviewing different offices and talking to their personnel. You must be compatible with them, since they will be spending your money and since communication with the various buyers in the office can eliminate many merchandising problems. Also, talk to other store owners using the office you are considering for their opinions on service and fashion sense. Finally, talk with manufacturers whose judgment you value. For the most part, the better-known offices are reputable people wanting you to succeed. I have known merchants who felt that they couldn't live without their resident office, and others who would not go near one.

I might suggest that in the beginning you belong to an office. As a rank amateur, you can get from them the knowledge you need. You sign only a one-year contract (or in some cases no contract at all), so you are not married to the office for life. If later you feel you can fly alone, drop them. If still later you feel the office can help your business, rehire them. I belonged to an office all the time I was in business.

The Industry and the Market

If you were to read some of our national fashion editors (who shall remain nameless), you would be led to believe that the entire fashion industry in America was located in one of two places: between Broadway and Eighth Avenue in New York, and in Europe. In today's marketplace there are more salable goods produced elsewhere than in the above two places. Yes, dear store-owners, there is a world of fashion west of the Hudson River!

Today, as never before—and still growing at a rapid pace —there are the *so-called* regional markets. I say *so-called* because they have long ceased to be regional in scope.

I would be remiss if at this point I did not give you the benefit of my years as a buyer in the *market*. It is obvious that you could just sit in your store and buy—yes, overbuy—all the goods you need or think you need. So why go to the expense of traveling, hotel rooms, etc., in order to attend these regional and national markets? The answers: information, education, and deals.

I have spoken of trade journals, media, and other sources of information important to the operation of your business. Probably the most honest and unbiased well of knowledge to be tapped is the opinion of your fellow buyers and merchants. You will be amazed to see just how much information can be learned from casual conversations over lunch and visiting showrooms. I am not ashamed to say that I used everyone I talked to at market as a guide to new resources and as a reference on the ability of manufacturers to perform. As with any other source of information, you have to judge the credibility of the people with whom you are talking.

As a new buyer in the market with limited (if any) knowledge of the various manufacturers and sales reps, it is important that you know something about them. Do they deliver on time? Do they ship as per sample? Are they what they seem to be? Are they priced right, or can you buy the same garment elsewhere for less money? One of the best ways to find answers to these questions is by listening to other buyers. Never be bashful—ask questions. I never met a buyer who did not consider him- or herself an authority on certain lines and with very little prodding was willing to tell all!

A final note on handling yourself with manufacturers: I had a young cousin come into our business fresh out of college. He was bright, articulate, and a fast learner. Today he is a successful merchant with several stores of his own.

The advice I gave him, lo these many years ago, before our first trip to New York, holds true today: "Do not try to impress any manufacturers with how much you know, because in five minutes they will know how much you *really* know. If you go in and say, I am a new buyer; will you help me?" they will kill themselves for you. If you come on *wise*, they can bury you."

Remember, most manufacturers *want* to see you succeed. They realize just how confusing a market trip can be to a novice. As you become more successful and climb the merchandise ladder, you will remember the ones who were helpful.

Market Areas

The major manufacturing and/or market areas in the United States are New York, California, and Texas, in that order. Narrowing it down to cities we mean New York City, Los Angeles, and Dallas.

Even though all three run the gamut of casual to dressy, the look and feel of these markets can vary greatly. American designers and manufacturers have long since passed the threshold to fashion maturity. To a great extent, the buying public has dictated this growth and change. No longer do America's fashion buyers look to Europe as Muslims look to Mecca. We learned long ago that what Paris designers make is not always the look that sells. This is not to say that American designers are not influenced to some extent by European styling, but this influence is becoming less important as our *native-born* talent grows in international acceptance.

Each of the three major market areas—New York, Los Angeles, and Dallas—has its own flavor. This difference is more than geographical, yet climate does play a role.

The manufacturers located in each area are somewhat influenced by the local merchant *princes* and *princesses*. Even though the major stores, and most of the smaller operations, buy goods manufactured in every market, the local manufacturers cater to the needs of those *locals* with big purchasing power and the regional specialty stores.

As an example: sales reps from New York are often quick to mention how well Bloomingdale's is doing with their goods; if they are from Los Angeles, the only thing that changes is the name of the store—The May Co., or the Broadway, while Dallas people are quick to mention Neiman Marcus. Yet, if the truth be known, a good style is a good style and sells almost anywhere.

I have been speaking of manufacturing centers. There are definite regional *selling* markets that overlap the major manufacturing centers. In addition to the three already mentioned, we have seen apparel marts grow up in Chicago, Atlanta, San Francisco, Miami, Charlotte, New Orleans, and Denver—and many minimarkets in smaller cities. Each of these centers has some manufacturing, but not in the degree that the big three do.

The largest single building in the world devoted exclusively to the showing and selling of apparel at wholesale is the Apparel Mart in Dallas. When originally built in 1964, it was 880,000 square feet. Since that time it has been enlarged to 1,800,000 square feet, with another 500,000 square feet under construction. Other cities with large apparel marts are Los Angeles and Chicago; Atlanta has recently completed its new mart. You have probably noticed that I have not mentioned New York. New York has no single building, but rather covers a large area known as the *garment district*. A comic once said, "The garment district in New York runs from 16th Street north to the Catskills in the summer and turns around and goes from 40th Street to Miami in the winter." Alright, so he exaggerated a little.

The main difference among the big three centers can be thought of in terms of their approach to fashion. New York is more *experimental* than the other two—quicker to pick up on fads. Los Angeles can at times get over-casual, with an emphasis on the sport look, while Dallas is a bit more conservative. As with any generalizations, I have left myself open to a lot of criticism—or, as we say in the garment industry, a lot of *g'shrying* (screaming).

Of course, not all manufacturers in each city fit the same

mold, but here again I have made a judgment based on my own perceptions after 25 years of going to these cities as a buyer and earning a *"girl-watcher"* medal by observing women on the streets.

Regional markets were a natural evolution based on a shifting and migratory population. With inflation and the heavy cost of traveling to New York, it became evident that buyers needed to have a place to shop nearer their homes. It is this same theory that helps create retail shopping centers. If you think of New York as *"downtown,"* then it is easy to imagine Los Angeles, Dallas, Chicago, Atlanta, etc., as your large regional shopping malls.

Using the same line of reasoning, we can more fully appreciate the influence exerted by the community in which the manufacturer is located, either consciously or subconsciously.

Making Deals

Making deals is a different story. As I have said previously, you are not Macy's and should not expect to be treated the same in any area, let alone that of making deals. To clarify this statement, I am speaking only of special merchandising deals and not of the way they should deal with you as a customer.

There are many different kinds of deals that can be made. If your town is small enough, you may be able to get an *exclusive* which means having the line alone in your town. If you are in a larger city where you cannot give the manufacturer enough business to tie up his line, then try for an exclusive on *certain numbers* in the line. This is called *working around* another store's numbers. All of this is determined by how important you feel this particular resource is to your business.

Some manufacturers are so anxious to sell you that they will come up with a *round trip* deal. What this means is simply that they ship you on memo (i.e., you do not own the goods), and in the event that this merchandise does not sell, you have the privilege of returning it to the factory within a specified period of time. On the face of it, you would think that this was a very good deal. But do not be lulled into a sense of false security by this offer. I was always leery of these types of offers for several reasons: the merchandise offered will seldom be the manufacturer's top numbers. And a busy resource that is performing well in the stores will never offer goods on memo, because it barely has enough production to cover legitimate orders. Lastly, you are not big enough for that manufacturer to realize enough future business to make deals of this type worthwhile for him. There may come a time when a sales rep feels so strongly about one or two numbers you wish to pass (not buy)—while buying other numbers in his line—that he will say, "Take this one, I own it." If this happens, make sure you have a notation on the order copy stating that this particular number is on "memo." And you should never return it if you have sold more than half of what you have received.

Another main area for "dealing" is in advertising allowances. Most arrangements call for *3 percent of purchases not to exceed 50 percent of space cost not including preparation costs.* This is not as confusing as it might appear at first reading. Example: You buy $5000 worth of goods; 3 percent equals $150. You are running an ad that is 60 inches @ $5 per inch for a total space cost of $300. One half of your space cost is $150, or the manufacturer's allowance to you.

I say *"most arrangements,"* since larger stores with more buying power can, and do, make better deals. There are times when a bigger user may demand set amounts toward an ad to be used at the store's discretion.

A fourth major area for the experienced buyer to get that little extra edge is in off-price (OP) goods. In the previous chapter we discussed the application of OP goods to offset markdowns. At this point I would like to attack this subject from another direction.

The actual purchasing of OP goods can make your reputation either as an astute buyer or as one who is unreasonable and unpleasant and to be avoided. The cardinal rule to remember here is: *a deal, to be a good deal, must be good for all parties involved.*

There are buyers who will offer a manufacturer of $29.75-to-$49.75 dresses $6 to $10. This is an example of a one-sided deal—*good only for the buyer.* A manufacturer may want $24.75 for his $29.75 garment, the reverse of the above and another one sided deal—*good only for the manufacturer.* A good deal is one where, after *pleasant* negotiations, you mutually arrive at a price where the manufacturer does not get hurt and you can sell at a profit.

Getting back to our previous discussion of reasons why you should spend the money for market trips: everything can be accomplished by speaking to someone at the *home office* who has more authority than the *road* salesperson calling on you in your store.

Four Criteria of the Industry

By nature, the apparel industry can be best described as a group of segmented manufacturers with a uniformity of intent. Their desire is to apply their combined talent to the four criteria that govern this industry: a saleable look, a good feel, the right price, and the proper fit.

Look runs the entire gamut from the most casual to the elegantly dressy, but it must always give the wearer an air of confidence that comes with being fashionably correct. Look can be ethnic in nature, loud or conservative, bright or subdued, a junior or a half-size, but it can't be uncomfortable in the customers' mind. When the wearer looks in the mirror, she must feel that she looks as good as she can with what nature gave her.

"*Feel*" is comfort—whether it covers what we said above about "look" or the weight of the garment. Obviously, a manufacturer who caters to customers in Buffalo will not sell the same goods in Miami. The fabrics used become important to the area. For you as a retailer, it becomes necessary that your inventory reflect the climate of your community.

Price within the context of the industry can be best summed up as "*Fashion is in your customers' eyes, not in their pocketbooks.*" We may have been brainwashed by *so-called* fashion writers into believing that for something to be *real* fashion, it has to be expensive. If you think that jeans are not fashion, go to any high school, college, or shopping center and see what women (or men) are wearing. This piece of the fashion scene can almost be called a uniform. True, it may not be *high* fashion in the truest sense of the word, but it is fashion nonetheless.

Fit, though left to last, is probably the most important factor. As every manufacturer and retailer knows, a good style in the right-weight fabric and in the season's number one color will not sell if the fit is wrong. If we look at the other three rules governing this industry, we find that *fit* bears on them all. The garment will not *look* good on the customer, the *feel* will be uncomfortable, and no *price* will sell it if the *fit* is wrong.

Now, let's review what we have covered in this chapter on sales reps and manufacturers. We know that manufacturers try to create saleable, fashion-right merchandise from which we can stock an inventory from which our customers can select goods to buy. We know that we can trust the good ones and should avoid the bad ones.

Ten

Advertising and Windows

What they see is what they get...
if you're an honest merchant!

Advertising is the image-creator for your store, a "necessary evil," a major expense item, or your most important selling tool—depending on whether you are speaking to a public relations agency, a lawyer, a CPA, or your commissioned salespeople. In truth, it is all of these and more.

Advertising, if used properly, can become your servant, your friend, your salesperson and the voice and face of your store. When misused or handled badly, it becomes a master, an enemy, and a competitor; worst of all, it says nothing.

If, as a small business owner, you are ever to be led down the primrose path, advertising can be a prime cause. How can this usual "business getter" be a traitor to your operation? The reason is quite simple. The fallacy usually found in this so-called asset is your overconfidence and faith in your ability to act as an advertising expert. Do not think that just because you read your competitors' ads, you can create ads suitable to your business.

America, more than any other country on earth, is in part a product of advertising. We buy soap, toothpaste, cars, toilet tissue, clothes, etc., based on what we are told by clever advertising agencies. We also *do not* buy specific products in the above categories because we are not sold by not-so-clever ad agencies. Because we are used to doing what the ad people tell us, we are doomed to thinking we can tell others what to do. Here again, *it ain't necessarily so!* Why is it that most small business people refer every problem of their business to the *experts*, and yet feel competent to guide and create in this most difficult area.

The formula is really simple: tell them what you have to sell, talk them into buying your wares, and keep your name in front of potential customers. Simple, right? Wrong!

Like many other *so-called* facts of life, advertising wears many different faces: newspapers, television, radio, direct mail, fliers, billboards, word-of-mouth, and windows. Each serves a different purpose yet is geared to accomplish the same end: to sell merchandise!

Let us examine each of the above in relation to the small store. The reason we will discuss small-store benefits is that large stores have the budget to employ them all, while you as a small merchant will be forced to make a choice between the various media because of limited funds to spend on advertising.

There are basically two types of advertising (note: *types*, not *means* or *media*); they are what I call *what* and *where*.

The *"what"* is directed at the customers who do not know what they want to buy; in fact, they do not even know that they are ready to buy. The ancient Chinese said, "A picture is worth a thousand words." Fashion advertising can elicit a desire for your merchandise through the picture of the garment.

We are probably the only industry in the world that sells a product that the government requires people to buy. What do I mean? There are laws against nudity, aren't there? If that's true, then consider this further truism: they may have to buy clothes, but they do not have to buy them from you.

With *"where"* advertising, our audience consists of customers who already know *"what"* they want but do not know *"where"* to buy it. Your job should be to convince them to buy it from you.

Now that we have clarified the *"whats"* and *"wheres,"* let's look at the means.

Newspaper

This is your best choice (along with TV) for showing fashion. Let us expand the old Chinese adage: *"A picture is worth a thousand words."* Adding, *"besides no one would read an ad that long."*

When considering a newspaper ad, there are several rules to follow:

1. *Insist on the best possible location in the paper for the type of merchandise you are selling.* As a small advertiser, it will be difficult for you to demand (and get) the front page of a section. The next spot is the back page of the section, but this too is probably confined to a major store. What you can insist on is page 2 or 3 of the proper section. I always preferred page 3 since customers who read the paper from front to back will see page 3 before page 2. What do I mean by the *proper* page? If you are selling womenswear, then you want the society sections (or *soc,* as we say). Menswear belongs either in the first section or in sports; cars belong in the classified, while furniture can run anywhere and usually does!

Be leery of special sections or supplements as they can cost more for no additional circulation. There are, from time to time, special deals by chargecard banks whereby they pick up part of the cost in a special section devoted to merchants and services accepting their cards. You will have to make the judgment as to what advantage this offers you and the extent of their participation.

Advantage can be an elusive factor. You must decide if being part of a section will benefit you more than appearing in a less crowded section where *your* customers may be used to looking, or expected to look, for your ad.

If the "plastic carders" (bank charges) offer a large enough participation in the cost, then you might want to consider taking advantage of the offer. However, if it is just a nominal rebate, then you must consider who will get the most benefit from your ad—you or the bank.

2. *There is no universal "right" day to run your ads.* This can be easily determined by reading the paper and noting which day carries the most ads by your competitors. You cannot use major stores as a guide since they will, for the most part, be in every day.

However, there are certain days that are usually accepted as "good," and with reason. One of these is the day before a late night (if an evening paper) or the morning of a late night. Friday is normally considered good in an evening paper since Saturday is the best retail day of the week.

Just as there are certain "right" days to run ads, there are certainly "wrong" days. For example, do not run ads in a Saturday evening paper. Since your store will probably be closed the next day (Sunday), your ad would be wasted.

3. *It is not the size of the ad, but how the space is used.* A small ad with a distinctive border, clever head, and well done artwork can do more to dominate a page than using half a page poorly. Copy is relatively unimportant. This last statement will draw angry cries of protest from all ad agency copywriters, but I would be disappointed if it didn't. Let us think this out to its realistic conclusion. What grabs readers first when they are skimming through the paper is the artwork. If it holds their attention for a split second, what now

must hold them? The head, that's what! All else working, they will now read the copy. It is at this point that the copy moves from a relatively unimportant position to a very important place in the ad. However, all else must be working for the ad first before the reader gets this far. If you buy what I have said, then it follows that your copy should be kept at an absolute minimum, since the average reader has a short attention span.

My ideal ad would be a composite of Macy's distinctive ragged border and Gimbel's charcoal artwork, combined with Neiman-Marcus copy.

As a small businessman I could not afford a high-priced advertising manager, an art director, and a clever copy-writer. So I hired them all for less than $1 per week. That's what it cost me to subscribe to the Sunday *New York Times*.

I do not believe that it is wrong to take advantage of every opportunity for small businesses to learn from the heavy hitters. There are no heavier hitters than the major stores in The Big Apple. Remember, there is a distinct difference between stealing and emulating.

4. *Your store name (logo or sig cut) should be done in a distinctive and unusual way, yet be easy to read.* The opposite of this theory is Lord & Taylor of New York and elsewhere, which has a logo that is nearly illegible, yet which is identifiable within the context of its ad because of the distinctive way in which its advertising is handled. Of course, they have spent a fortune over many years in creating this name identification.

The script (artwork) in which you do your logo is important, since you will use it as a main tool in forming customer identification with your store. Once you have arrived at one you like, it should be used on *all* your bags, boxes, books, and stationery—and anywhere else your name appears in print.

5. *If your town has more than one newspaper, check their circulation very carefully.* You must check for more than just how many papers they deliver: *to whom* are they delivered? You will find that one is more nearly geared to your class of customers. As an old rule of thumb, an evening paper is better for a low-to-moderate income clientele, while a morning paper serves the more affluent customer. The reasoning behind this theory is that the working people who get up early and go to work, have perhaps no time to read a paper in the morning, while the customers who have the time to look over the ads while drinking their morning coffee are the supposed buyers of the "better" goods.

Applying this to your advertising budget, it becomes logical to run your sales in the evening along with your moderate-priced merchandise, but a better garment at a higher price should be in the morning paper. You will also find that one paper has a wider distribution than the other. If one of your papers covers a large portion of the county and state, then it should be used for any mail-order ads you may wish to run, regardless of the above considerations.

This whole theory means nothing if we were to use New York City or any large metropolitan center where many people are forced to commute an hour or more by train or other form of public transportation and therefore have the time to read a morning paper.

6. *Rates are not the same for all newspapers.* Most will offer discounts based on multiple insertions. What this means is the more times you run ads, the cheaper the *"per line"* rate becomes. Newspaper advertising is sold by the line, not the inch. Ads are prepared by the inch, but the charge is a line cost. Thus an ad that is 2 × 8 means that it is 2 columns wide and 8 inches high. Since there are 14 lines to the column inch, you have an ad of 224 lines. If your cost is .55 per line, you have just spent $123.20. Here again, as in the earlier discussion regarding supplies, don't buy more than you need.

7. *Do not be disappointed if you do not get immediate results from a fashion ad.* A straight, regular-price ad seldom gives you the impact that you will get from a *sale* ad. An inexpensive *mail-order* ad yields more directly related sales than most other types of ads you can run. The best two advertising words are *sale* or *free.* Obviously, not every day can be sale day or you will destroy your fashion image. The exception these days seems to be in the coat department, where you will seldom see a regular-price ad. However, even a sale ad can be done in good taste. If you are not a discounter or cheap operation, where the only thing that counts is the price, then even your clearance ads can be done in such a manner as not to detract from your fashion image. Cute headings and clever artwork do much to add to the ad's impact while keeping it *"clean* and neat."

8. *Check your proof carefully.* After you have submitted your ad to the paper, and before it is to run, the newspaper will bring you a *proof.* This is an exact copy of the way your ad will look in the paper, and it gives you an opportunity to check for misspelled words, proper pricing, store hours, sizes, colors, etc. Remember, once you have seen the proof, the responsibility for the way your ad looks and reads is yours. Once you have been shown a proof, and you have *approved* it, you have relieved the paper of that responsibility, and you have no one to blame for any mistakes except yourself. However, if you have made corrections on your proof and the paper has failed to remedy its mistakes, then you have recourse. That recourse can be anything from a discount to rerunning the ad at *no charge,* depending on the seriousness of the error.

9. *The cardinal sin in all advertising is to have an ad run and not have the merchandise in stock.* This is no one's fault but yours. Never plan an ad based on when you are supposed to receive the goods from the manufacturer. That kind of advance planning can cause nothing but heartaches.

Advertised merchandise should be highlighted in your windows and spotted on the selling floor. If for some inexcusable reason you do not have, or are not adequately covered by, the advertised goods at least six days before the ad is scheduled to run, then cancel the ad and replace it with another item. But don't just grab any old item to fill the space. The substitute garment should be as timely and important as the one it is replacing. It is better to run nothing than to run the wrong item.

After your ad has run, it should be posted on a bulletin board for all your salespeople and customers to see. The way this is handled in most stores is to have a free-standing frame, usually a little larger than a full newspaper page, on which to display your current ads. Do not let an ad stay on the board for more than a week, and in no case should one ad overlap another. Nothing looks worse than a messy board full of old ads. Remember, each ad cost you money and should be treated like a diamond. Just as you would not let a dress look sloppy in stock, so you should not let your advertising center (the board) in your store be less than perfect.

Television and Radio

Television

Television is a fantastic form of advertising—*if you can afford it!* This particular *"if"* only you can judge. If you watch TV with an eye for the ads, you will rarely see anything smaller than a major department store using this medium, and this is usually a *"co-op"* (vendor participation) ad. There may be an occasion to use a tie-in with a product line that has bought your area. What this means is that a major manufacturer has bought certain market areas around the country to run ads simultaneously. A good example of this type of advertising is the Johnny Carson Show. If it is a product that you carry, the station can run your logo on the screen during the showing of the spot. This can usually be done at a greatly reduced rate, since there are no preparation costs for you to bear. If the price is right ("right" meaning within your budget) and the product line is important within your store and you have the particular item in stock, then you may wish to spend for the tie-in. Remember, even at a bargain rate, it will still cost more than a normal ad elsewhere, so consider it carefully.

You will note that I am not devoting much space to television even though it is an important medium. The reason is: important to whom? You would not be reading this book unless you intended to open a *small* store, and I feel that small stores with their limited budgets cannot afford TV, except under very certain circumstances. A more appropriate consideration, therefore, is radio.

Radio

Radio can be used most effectively, but I never found it desirable for selling *fashion*. It is difficult, if not impossible, to describe a garment with justice in 30 to 60 seconds. We always used radio for special events, such as sales, where we were selling price rather than specific merchandise.

As with newspapers and television, "position" is important. I believe the best time for your message is during what radio people call *drive time*. This is from 6:30 to 9:00 A.M. and from 3:30 to 6:00 P.M. What you are obviously shooting for here is the car radio; and this, of course, is geared to the adult audience. If your store caters to a young group, then you will want to consider *dressing* time (7 to 8 A.M.) or *homework* time (early evening or late—after 10 P.M.).

Almost every town today, no matter how small, has more than one radio station. It can therefore seem a puzzle as to which station to buy. As with newspapers, there are stations that will reach the audience you seek in the best possible way. Every station in town will show you its so-called *independent* surveys boasting its percentage of the audience. The surveys can be much like political polls: it depends on whose poll you read. I am not saying that they are deliberately misleading; what I am saying is that you can make numbers do anything you wish. So take all polls with a grain of salt. The best way is to run your own survey with your own customers. Instruct your salespeople and office help to ask all those coming into the store what radio station, TV channel, or newspaper they use, and this will give you a truer picture of your particular audience.

Returning to the idea of radio for special events: what is more special than a Grand Opening? If you are opening a new store, you may wish to consider more than one station, since you will have had no time to do your own survey. However, keep in mind the type of store you are operating: young or mature? This will eliminate some stations and may relieve you of some of the confusion.

Billboards

If I had worked my ad budget and selected *all* other forms of advertising that I intend to use and still have money left over, then I might consider billboards. Chances are I would even then talk myself out of it.

Billboards serve a purpose in some businesses, but with the rapid changes that occur in the world of fashion, I feel that it would be too difficult to keep this medium current.

Another disadvantage to a small store using billboards as a form of advertising is the cost. Today's high costs make it doubly important that we spend our advertising dollars as carefully as possible, with an eye to the greatest return. Billboards do not give that return.

The speed of automobiles is another factor against the use

of billboards. When I was young the company that put bill-boards to their fullest use was the Burma Shave Company. Their small signs placed at intervals along the highway were a source of delight to the traveler. As the speed of the automobile increased, the effectiveness of this form of advertising decreased, and today it has been totally discontinued.

I have saved for the last the three forms of advertising that I consider the most important: windows, word-of-mouth, and direct mail.

Windows

I was once told by a very astute merchant that if he only could keep one form of advertising, it would be his windows. His rationale was that with all other forms of advertising, customers have to make an effort to come to your store. With windows, the customers are standing at the store when they see your merchandise, and they merely have to walk in the front door. Carrying this theory to its fullest, this merchant never allowed the front door of his store to be closed "Nothing should make it difficult for the customer to enter." In this day of high energy costs, I feel it is wiser to keep the air conditioning or heat *in the store and not cool or warm the sidewalk outside.* But assuming that your windows are very important—and why not assume it?—then the time, effort, and money spent on them are also very important.

Proper backgrounds should enhance—not detract—from the merchandise. There are *five* seasons a year: spring, summer, fall/winter, and holiday. With minor alteration of the major backgrounds, you will reflect Easter, Mother's and Father's Day, Thanksgiving, Clearance Sales, Back-to-School, etc. This is usually done with signs—but here again, don't overdo it. Even a sale sign can be done in good taste.

Backgrounds can be purchased from fixture/display firms;

most larger cities have one or more firms specializing in these items. People in the display business are usually well informed and can assist you in the proper size and type based on your store, its image, and the size of your windows. Like buying any other supply, you can spend as much as you want. Your windows should have "couth," but they need not cost a fortune. After you have changed seasons and purchased new backgrounds, take the old ones out carefully and wrap them for next year. You will be surprised what some new foliage or a little paint can do to make last year's fixtures look new and different. Reworking them is a lot cheaper than buying new ones!

The amount of goods you put in your windows has a direct bearing on the image you wish to project. It is not necessary to carry half of your inventory *"behind glass."* This look is indicative of a cheap operation. The only exception to the amount of goods shown could be a junior jean operation, where a variety of tops and jeans is shown; even then, it should be done in a cute and attractive way. Moderate-to-better stores should treat each garment as though it were a gem. *Make sure that every piece you display is clean, properly pressed, and color coordinated.*

Always color coordinate the merchandise in the window. Present a complete package of garment and accessories, as this becomes another selling tool for your salespeople. If your customer is already half sold before entering the store, it can mean extra sales for you. If your store is to be important to the community—and more importantly, to your customers—you must *teach fashion.* Your customers will look to you for guidance, and your windows are *always* teaching, even when the store is closed.

Ask yourself two questions before you select goods for the window: *what's hot (timely)?* and *what's wanted?* It always behooves you to show your newest merchandise. Windows should also reflect blends of the currently *right* color in as many representative departments as possible *without over-crowding.*

Although there may be times when you are limited in your newspaper ads, you are never limited in your windows. You can change the merchandise in your windows as often as you wish. I always insisted that my store managers have their windows changed at least twice a week—on Monday and Thursday, as this covered the weekends, both coming and going: most of the customers came in on Saturday, and I did not want them to see the same goods in the windows on two consecutive Saturdays. If I had but one day a week to trim windows, it would be Thursday. This does not preclude putting in something new (a single item) at *any* time—every day, if necessary.

Your mannequins should be kept in good repair—with wigs combed and chipped paint restored—and generally looking as good as they can. It is important that the window carpet be swept before putting in new merchandise; and remember that your customers can't see the goods through dirty glass—keep it washed! Never, but *never,* have burned-out lights in your show windows. In addition to the dimness, they detract from the overall image you are trying to create.

Only a very involved discussion could attempt to tell you how to rig a mannequin, how to drape merchandise on the floor or from fixtures, or when to show certain goods. I can teach you this very simply: go to school on your competitors; window-shop the other stores in town, and when you see a particularly good window, make notes. If you have a bad memory, sketch it. I wouldn't suggest that you do this during store hours; your competition may not particularly care for this form of flattery.

To emphasize this point let me tell you what my buyers and I used to do on trips to New York. We would always travel on Sunday so as not to miss a working day on either end of the trip. We would always arrive in New York between three and five on Sunday afternoon. After checking into the hotel and unpacking, we would head straight for Fifth Avenue with a notebook and sketch pad. We would walk and look. When a good window presented itself, we would sketch; or, if it was just a clever sign, we would write down the copy. In this way, we had the advantage of the best display brains in the world. Not everything we sketched was adaptable to our operation, but variations on the theme usually worked. The added advantage to this was that we were not *borrowing* from competitors.

Word of Mouth

Good or bad, this form of advertising you earn and cannot buy. The way you treat customers, the selectivity of your stock, the cleanliness of your store, and the policies that govern your operation establish what people will say about you.

None of us wants to be bad-mouthed, and we would all like to have nothing but friends and no enemies. The trick is to have ninety-nine people saying something good about you so that the one unhappy customer will appear to be exactly what he or she is—one unhappy customer in a hundred.

Nothing in this world replaces a smile and courtesy when dealing with the public. We all like to be treated royally when spending our hard-earned money. The proof of the pudding is to ask an out-of-towner about his visit to New York, and listen to the tales of rudeness. New York—but not all New Yorkers—has a reputation for being curt, lacking patience, and being generally rude. Deserved or not, word-of-mouth has hung this mantle on our largest city. If word of mouth can do this to an entire city, think of what can be done to one small store. The results could be disastrous.

Word of mouth goodwill can be generated in many different ways, most of which may seem small and insignificant: a pleasant greeting when the customer enters the store; not making the customer wait too long for service; always having the advertised article; answering the phone promptly; keeping a clean store (especially the rest rooms); participation in civic events; serving coffee or soft drinks; and above all, courtesy, a smile, and service.

Direct Mail

This is the most positive way of getting your store's message into the homes that you consider important—your immediate shopping area; and for the most part, you can feel assured that it is read. Let us examine this means of advertising a little closer.

First of all, the average return (the number of customers you can expect to come into the store from reading your mailer) is about 3–5 percent. Giveaway sales can result in a higher return; thus if you mailed 5000 pieces, you could expect approximately 150 to 250 *lookers*. (Not everyone who comes in will be a *buyer*.) This means that 4750 to 4850 threw your mailer in the trash. Secondly, the post office hates "junk" mail. You may feel that your mailer is a work of art, but to the postman who has to carry it on his back, it's "junk." Therefore, the cost of mailing has been steadily increasing, and today it has become an expensive vehicle based on return. Along with the cost of postage, printing, and preparation, mailer costs have also increased. But under certain circumstances, direct mail is still an effective way to advertise; these "certain circumstances" include: store sales, catalogues, special events, etc. Under these conditions you should enjoy a much greater return than the 3 percent if the event is strong enough.

My own preference is for the largest size postcard the post

office will permit for my direct-mail piece instead of a folded letter in an envelope. I feel a customer has to read it since it is open; and besides, it is much cheaper to prepare and mail.

Another form of direct mail, which is *not* mailed, is the *flyer*. This is the form of advertising that is usually found behind the doorknob at your home or under your windshield wiper. A flyer is relatively inexpensive and can be quite productive. Your principal problem will be one of distribution. There are services you can contract for that will hand deliver by selected streets in the exact trading area that is best for your store. Always use a professional service for the best results. Some people use high school students to go from door-to-door; however, the danger here is that the flyers may not get delivered at all. Many a circular has been thrown down a sewer, and the store never knows. If you have teenagers in the family, this is a good job for them.

As with anything else, when looking for a service to do this for you, shop the price, as it can vary greatly from one to another.

A flyer is prepared in much the same manner as any other direct piece of mail with the exception that your production cost should be considerably lower. The grade of paper will be of a cheaper quality, and the printing can be done by a less expensive printing method. Nonetheless, your flyer can be very effective if handled properly. Like newspaper and radio, which require preparation, using direct mail presents a dual question: whom do you mail to and where do you get a mailing list? A mailing list can be had from various sources:

1. You can use a mailing service that will pinpoint the section of town and class of customer you wish to attract. This can be expensive, and if you decide to use a service of this type, be sure to shop price as it will vary.
2. Contact your newcomers' Welcome Wagon.
3. Sometimes the utility companies offer a service that can be helpful.

4. X-Cross directory (listing of addresses and phone numbers —streets in alphabetical order; phones by exchange), or your City Directory. If you are using a City Directory, list the streets you wish to canvass and tear out the pages. Hire a few high schoolers to address the desired streets.

Budgeting Your Advertising

Advertising should be strictly budgeted. Most stores will allow 2–5 percent of expected sales for this expenditure. Department stores allow for a smaller budgeted percentage. This is logical; a store doing millions in sales can allow .5 to 1 percent and still dominate the media. You as a small operator must use a higher percentage figure just to get some coverage.

How much should I spend?

The amount of money you will allocate on advertising will be affected by the following factors:

1. Expected sales for the budgeted month. These sales will depend on the special events coming up in that month, such as Mother's Day, Father's Day, Easter, Christmas, etc.
2. Store Location. If you are in a free-standing building, and must attract every customer by the strength of your individual advertising, you will naturally spend more than if you were in a regional mall with everyone else running ads.
3. How long you have been in business. A well-established store will need to spend less than a new store since it will have built up customer identification.
4. The size of your trading area. If you are in a relatively small trading area, you will spend less than in a large metropolitan city. You will be reaching fewer people; therefore, your cost should be lower. Media costs, of course, will be lower in small towns.
5. Your competition. This will also have a relationship to the amount you budget for advertising—it is the one place where keeping up with the Joneses is not altogether bad. This is, of course, if the Jonses aren't totally overspending.

Budgeting your advertising dollars is as important as budgeting any other expense item. Never forget, an advertising budget is only a guide and must be kept flexible.

In order to keep control on advertising expenses I maintained an advertising calendar. At the end of each month I would estimate my sales for the coming month. I used 3 percent of estimated sales as my advertising budget. Since I knew my cost per inch of newspaper space, I would then divide my cost into the budget to arrive at the number of inches to be used. If that particular month were to have a direct-mail piece, or if I planned some use of radio, I would subtract the amount of those expenses from the budget before dividing by my newspaper cost.

Example: Planned volume $25,000; 3 percent of estimated sales = $750; cost of newspaper space $5 per inch. Therefore I had 150 inches to use in the paper (see p.139).

This calendar served as a reference guide the following year. Before planning what ads I would run, I would go back to the previous year's calendar to see what I had run to create the volume figures I was trying to meet.

In addition to the calendar, I kept a scrapbook of all ads and direct-mail pieces I had used. In some cities, the newspaper will supply you with a scrapbook free of charge. Your ads should be placed in the book in chronological order with the name of the paper and the date run. If you add information such as the weather conditions on the day the ad ran and the amount of sales generated by the ad, you will have a relatively inexpensive record of how well your advertising is performing.

I have tried to cover the major forms of media use. There are others, but to a small store they are not applicable. You can't do everything the heavy hitters do, but what you do, do well and in good taste, and the customers will come to you. What more can you ask of your advertising?

ADVERTISING CALENDAR

April

S	M	T	W	T	F	S
			1 10" ABC DRESS STYLE 361	2	3 16" XYZ SUIT STYLE 480	4 26"
5	6	7	8 12" DEF DRESS STYLE 1218	9	10 16" GH DRESS STYLE 930	11 28"
12	13	14	15 12" JK SUITS STYLE 1018	16	17 18" PRE-EASTER SALE GOOD FRIDAY	18 30"
19 18" AFTER- EASTER SALE PALM SUNDAY EASTER 1ST DAY OF PASSOVER	20	21	22 12" AFTER- EASTER SALE SECRETARIES DAY	23	24 18" AFTER- EASTER SALE EASTERN ORTHODOX HOLY FRIDAY	25 54"
26 EASTERN ORTHODOX EASTER	27	28	29 MEG- SPTS WEAR STYLES 1150 ✓ 840	30		/150

EST. VOL. $25,000.00

3% = $750.00
5% = $1250.00

RATE: $5.00 PER INCH

INCHES TO SPEND 150

3% = 150"
5% = 250"

Advertising Your Grand Opening

When opening a new store, the first ad you will run will be a Grand Opening Sale. It is with this ad that your image is first projected to the buying public. It is here that you take your first big step toward being a successful merchant. It is here that you take your first shot directly at the audience you hope to hit. *Give this ad much thought and concentrated effort.*

For your *opening* you may wish to use more than one medium. In order of importance (after the windows, of course) choose newspaper, then direct mail, followed by radio. Your message must not only tell your story but also offer some incentive to bring the customer into the store. It is here that the words *sale* and/or *free* (the two most powerful words in advertising) come into play.

A special *Grand Opening Sale* offering reduced prices on well-established items or a *"free gift "* for "just coming in to see us, no purchase necessary" can be used effectively. You must be careful when marking down name-brand items for this event as you do not want to lose a resource because you are selling their goods too cheaply. Most manufacturers will give you a garment that can be used as part of a give-away wardrobe. Remember: if you don't ask, you don't get. So keep this event in mind when placing your opening orders.

If handled properly, your opening should generate traffic in your store. This will automatically create two classes of people: those who buy and those who do not—a ridiculously simple statement but think about it in this light: both groups are important, since they are people who took the time and effort to come into the store, and *they now know where you are located.*

It is important that you make the best possible use of these customers and potential customers. Have everyone coming in fill out a registration card with name, address, Zip, and phone number. This card can be used for a drawing to select the winner of your free wardrobe. A thank-you note can then be sent for having come into the store and now inviting them back. Put in its simplest terms, you are showing them that you appreciated their coming into your new store and that you are really interested in having their business.

There are many special events during the year that normally call for, or can be used as, an excuse for an advertised *sale*. This use of special events can be overdone, and then you have created a monster: customer is reluctant to buy anything at regular price. So be careful.

Let us look at what has become an all-too-familiar way of advertising:

January:	Clearance Sale
February:	Final Clearance Sale
March:	Pre-Easter Sale
April:	After-Easter Sale
May:	Mother's Day Sale
June:	Father's Day Sale and/or Pre July 4th Sale
July:	After July 4th Sale
August:	Back-to-School Sale
September:	Final Clearance (summer), Early Fall Sale
October:	Halloween Sale
November:	Pre-Thanksgiving Sale
	After-Thanksgiving Day Sale (but hurry, you have only 5 days)
December:	Pre-Christmas Sale
	After-Christmas Sale
January:	It starts all over again!

This schedule works well for department stores. So that you will not think I am arguing with success, let me be quick to say that majors can get away with the above. Their advertising budgets are so large that they can be running regular-price ads at the same time as their sales, so that they do not create quite as bad a monster as you would, where your entire schedule would be sale-time.

However, there *are* key sale days, and do not overlook the advantage of using them. Clearances at the end of a season (summer and winter), after July 4th, and after Thanksgiving Day are but a few—and last but not least, there is your Anniversary Sale. The time of this sale has little, if anything, to do with when you actually opened your front doors. It has probably never occurred to you, but most stores run their anniversary sales in a good selling month, such as October or November. There is never a reason to run a sale except when customers are ready to buy.

As a merchant with a new store, your biggest problem after location, lease, and money will be getting customers into your store. This chapter has dealt with the most important tool you have for doing this—advertising.

Much of the retail advertising that we see does not accomplish the job it is set out to do. Either the timing, the coverage, or the conception is handled badly. It is important that as much concentrated effort be applied in this area as in any other part of your business.

If I could leave you with but one thought in reference to advertising it would be this: *keep it honest*. Nothing is more important than honesty in *everything* connected with the running of your business, and this holds particularly true in advertising.

Eleven

Selling

Merchandise is not like wine...
it doesn't get better with age...
sell it!

With this chapter we have reached the so-called nitty-gritty, the crux, the apex, the paramount part of this whole book: SELLING!

Up to this point you have picked a good location, signed a lease, arranged your financing, bought the fixtures and put them into your beautifully designed store, worked your open-to-buy, learned to work with sales reps, purchased your merchandise (which you have received and hung into stock on the right hangers), and planned your opening ads.

Now what?

You've got to sell it—that's what!

All that you have done has been mere preparation for the moment you open your front door and the first customer walks into the shop. How they are greeted is the beginning of their relationship with your store.

Hiring and Salarying Your Saleshelp

What was said in Chapter 6 bears repeating at this time: a common mistake is hiring the cheapest possible help you can get. This is one place where you really get what you pay for. When hiring salespeople, keep the following in mind:

(1) *Employment application and interview:* Your first step, even before the face-to-face interview, is the employment application. This may sound simple, but because of government regulations it has become a complicated procedure. As an owner/manager, you will want to consult your attorney for current information as to what, and what not, you may ask a prospective employee. But a rule of thumb might well be: *if it's got nothing to do with the job, it isn't worth the risk of asking.*

Example: If you are interviewing a woman for a sales position, do not ask her if she can type. You may ask applicants where they live, but not their country of origin; whether they are American citizens, but, if they say no, not what their nationality is; whether they have ever been convicted of a criminal offense, but not if they have ever been arrested; whether they speak a foreign language, but not where they learned it. And remember: no questions regarding age, or you leave yourself open for an age discrimination suit.

Basically these rules serve a worthwhile purpose and the intent of the government is beyond reproach. It is the extent to which the matter has grown that makes compliance at times seem difficult. One way to learn what you need to know is to be a good listener, keeping questions open-ended ("*Why* do you think you'd be a good salesperson?" instead of "*Do* you think you'd be a good salesperson?"). If you keep the interview relaxed and conversational, the applicant will tell your more than you need to know.

After they are working for you, it's a whole new ball game. You are then permitted to ask for certain restricted information such as pertains to insurance, Social Security, and like matters that you were not previously allowed to ask about.

(2) *Appearance:* People who sell fashion should look fashionable. Certainly their appearance should not be a repudiation of your store's image. A salesperson should be to some extent an advertisement for good taste and good clothes, which translates into being an advertisement for the store, and someone whose advice on fashion and clothes customers will respect. In brief, a salesperson should *look* the part.

(3) *Do they come with a "book"?* What this means is do they have a "call trade"—customers of their own, established over the years while they were working for someone else? Can they call on these customers to come to your store because they now work for you? This kind of help is hard to come by, but it can be very important to a new store. A salesperson with a "book" cannot be overpaid.

(4) *Age is relatively unimportant:* Salespersons can perhaps be too young, but it is rare that they can be too old. Of course, some people's ideal might be a 20-year-old with 30 years of experience. Since this is obviously impossible, how about a 50-year-old who has the 30 years of experience and moves and acts like a 20-year-old?

(5) *Salary is a necessary evil:* You can't even get relatives to work for nothing—or should I say *especially* relatives? Anyway, you *do* have to pay them or they will quit. The manner and system of paying salespeople vary from store to store. There is *straight salary, salary plus commission,* and *salary against commission.* These different means arrive at different ends.

With *straight salary,* the employee receives a set amount each week, every two weeks, or monthly. In the retail business, it is usually a weekly salary. Weekly pay ordinarily applies to part-time help and non-selling people. The rate of pay at this level is for the most part determined by your competitors. It is therefore important that you find out what other stores of your size are paying their people and at least match their scale. You do not have to beat it, just be the same.

Salary against commissions means exactly that and applies to selling help. You pay a base salary that is subtracted at the end of each pay period from the commissions earned.

Example: you are paying a salary, or draw, of $150 per week. If this salesperson is working on 5 percent of sales, he or she must sell a minimum of $3000 per week to break even ($150 = 5% of $3000). If only $2000 is sold, at 5 percent the commissions would total $100—or $50 less than the draw. Most stores do not charge this deficit to the next week's draw; however, if a salesperson goes too many weeks of drawing more than he or she earns on commissions, the boss will be looking for a replacement. One great advantage to this system is that you know that your salespersons cannot cost you more than 5 percent if they make their quota or as much over it as they can.

On *salary plus commission*, the base salary is less since you are going to pay commissions on everything the salesperson sells. Of course, the commission rate is smaller, too. Example: The draw paid is $122.50 ($3.35 per hour) for a 35-hour week. If you give 2 percent on everything sold, then on sales of $2000 in one week, the salesperson gets a commission of $40, or a combined salary of $162.50. This salesperson is now costing you 8.12 percent instead of 5 percent. The biggest pitfall under this system can be a lack of incentive. If salespersons know that they will get commissions without maximum effort and that this will not affect their job security, they may not try their best, even though larger earnings can result from higher sales.

(6) *Morale:* A broad definition of this elusive factor might be the working relationship of your employees toward you and your store.

We have been taught in recent times that happy workers are more productive workers. As a store-owner, it becomes your job to keep them happy. Money, though important, is not the total answer. *Concern*, I believe, is of even greater importance—concern not only for their working conditions but also for their needs as individuals.

Dealing with Your Customer

Even *old dogs* can be taught new tricks, or at least reminded of what they should already know. The first contact a salesperson has with the customer entering the store is the most important. The entire relationship between that customer and your store is established by the greeting the customer receives and the length of time it takes someone to recognize the fact that he or she has walked through the front door.

Segal's rule: never let a customer come into the store and wander around without being greeted by someone. Even if everyone is busy, have your people trained to say, "Hello, we'll be with you in a moment" or "Can I show you where your sizes are?" The customer whom they are with will not resent this short interruption and will probably even appreciate the courtesy shown to a fellow shopper. Even if your store isn't busy, never permit salespeople to continue a conversation between themselves and delay greeting the customer. Remember, the only shot you have at that customer is while he or she is in the store. Your salespeople can finish their conversation some other time; and anyway, it's rude.

The initial greeting should not be, "May I help you?" The answer to this question can too easily be, "No, I'm just looking." Never ask a question that can have a negative replay. Selling must always be done from the *positive*. A better approach would be, "Hello, how are you today? Let me show you our new _____ we have just received." Customers not interested in that particular item may nevertheless feel inclined to tell you what they *do* want.

Important: If you know the customer's name, use it! There is nothing more flattering to anyone than being recognized by name. This is just simple human nature. Everyone likes to feel important, and believe me, your customer is the most important person in the world when shopping in your store.

Salespeople should be well trained in the art of *suggestive* selling. I say *art* since there is a fine line between, on the one hand, aiding customers or suggesting additional merchandise to complete their outfit or reminding them of something they may have forgotten and, on the other hand, *PRESSURE* selling. Segal's key rule here is that if you show a customer three garments, you sell one; if you show six or seven garments, you will probably sell none. *Never confuse the customer.*

No one wants to be pressured; the attempt may well be resented. However, a gentle nudge can be helpful to a customer and result in a larger sale for the salesperson and the store. Example: The customer is in the dressing room and you know that the dress she is considering will fit better with the proper bra and look better with the proper scarf and jewelry. The additional items should be brought to the customer (in the dressing room) and the outfit put together. A man is trying on a sport coat, and the pants he is wearing do not match. Suggest he try on the proper-colored slacks for a better perspective and, more likely than not, he will buy the slacks. With menswear customers, it is usually true that if you can get a man to try on the pants, he'll buy. This is merely suggestive selling, not pressuring.

The Dressing Room

A better name for a dressing room should be a *selling room*. This is the only place in the store that a salesperson can talk to a customer on a one-to-one basis with no one else listening and one of the best places to sell that additional merchandise. While on the subject of dressing rooms, certain rules should become a way of life with you and your salespeople:

1. Never permit more than three garments in the dressing room at one time. If the customer wants to see more, take one or two garments out before bringing in the additional ones. This serves two purposes: (a) it eliminates an element of confusion, and (b) it affords greater control over shoplifting.

2. After leaving the dressing room, never allow hangers, pins, tissue paper, tags, or trash to be left in there for the next customer to find, and above all never leave a garment. A garment doesn't sell hidden in a back dressing room but must be in stock for the next customer to find.

3. Every dressing room should have at least one small chair, a full-length mirror, spindle (garment hook) and an ashtray. You may not approve of (or condone) smoking, but some of your customers may, so provide a place for them to put their cigarettes other than on the floor. The mirror must *always* be clean and free of smudges and fingerprints. This is the duty of the salespeople if your budget does not permit a cleaning person. A full-length mirror becomes a selling tool since it helps keep the customer in the dressing room while you bring in your suggestive merchandise. A chair is for the customer's convenience and comfort, while the spindle is there obviously to hang their own clothes on plus the other garments your customer wants to try.

4. From time to time your vendors will give you signs advertising their goods. If you wish to feature these by posting them in your dressing room, that's fine, but do not put up more than one at a time. Too many signs in a small dressing room will give it a cluttered look. Always make sure that these signs are timely. Such signs as "Just Right for Spring" should not still be up in September, and a "Back-to-School" message in October is completely out of place. If you put one up, make sure it's up! Do not let one corner come loose and sag.

Service and Personal Attention

    These four rules can be summed up in one word: service. This is the main commodity you have to sell. What makes the small specialty store different, and gives it a reason to exist, is *service*.

    The major department stores, with their hundreds of sales-people, department managers, supervisors, and executives, cannot—and do not—offer the customer the personal attention and service that the small store can and does. How many times have you walked into a large store ready to buy and could not get anyone to wait on you? I recently went shopping with my wife and daughter. We selected our own merchandise and carried it to the cash stand ourselves, only to find three young people engrossed in a conversation and totally ignoring us. It was not until I said, "Do you work here?" that one of them came over to me and wrote up our purchase. Never, never, *never* permit this to happen in your store!

    I cannot stress service too greatly. It is a fact of life that large department stores will offer a larger selection in any given department than you can ever hope to offer. They will offer certain services (e.g. charge accounts, delivery) that you may not offer. Therefore, you must make your customers comfortable and service them to the best of your ability. There will always be those customers who do not wish to be rushed, who like to serve themselves, be recognized by name when entering the store, and generally be made to feel important. Therein lies the *raison d'etre* of the specialty store and why it will never disappear—so long as there are good merchants.

    In defense of the large stores it should be said that many of their problems in this area are difficult, if not impossible, to resolve. The department managers, who should be running their little half-acre, are often so bogged down with paper work that they cannot watch their floors properly. Because of the sheer weight of numbers (department stores have a great deal of traffic), the help cannot get to every one. Also, much of their selling force is part-time, who may care more about coffee breaks, getting in their time, when they get off, their date for that night, a school test for the next day, etc.. Their minds may not be on their work or the welfare of the store. Even though top management is aware of this problem, there may be little they an do to improve the situation.

Hopefully, there will be times when your store will be so busy that the immediate servicing of the customer will be difficult. At that point, offer a simple "I'll be with you in a moment. Won't you have a cup of coffee or a Coke?" When accompanied by a smile, this will do much to make the customer's wait more pleasant and seem shorter. Never allow your customers to get the impression that they are being ignored.

Educating Your Saleshelp

As we shall see in Chapter 12, there are many records that you will have to keep, some of which will aid you in buying, among other things. One of these is your "check-out" book. Your salespeople can perform a vital service in this area if they are trained to report immediately check-out (sales) of merchandise recently received and do not make you wait two or three days to find out through your normal posting channels. If you receive five pieces of a style and on the first day sell three, your salesperson should notify you at once. This type of selling record calls for a reorder, which should be telephoned in or mailed that day. The quicker you reorder, the sooner you have more to sell.

The same holds true if your salespeople are receiving specific requests for merchandise that you do not have in stock. Do not be misled by the isolated request; there must be a significant number of requests before you actually buy the item in question. After receiving consistent customer requests, be sure that your salespeople obtain all the specific information they can (e.g. price, color, manufacturer, where they saw it) and then you go look at it in the store mentioned. If what the customers want is more general in nature, such as "red sweaters," then buy the best red sweaters the market has to offer.

It is important to observe and to "shop" your competition yourself. However, your salespeople should be trained to do the same whenever they are in another store. Your competitors should be checked for in-store promotions, prices, windows, advertised items, and anything they seem to have in depth in their stock. Here again, specifics are important: get the manufacturer's name, the style number, price, etc., whenever possible.

Never forget that, as the boss, you are the focal point for the gathering of this data, sifting the wheat from the chaff and making the final decisions as to proper trends, items, and general customer reactions. All of this must be done accurately and with the least amount of delay. Also, as a buyer, you will be looking at many lines while at market, some of which you will not buy; but everything you see and hear, a good portion of which will come from conversation with other merchants, adds to your education in the best possible way to buy for, and run, your business. It then behooves you to pass on all pertinent information to your store people upon your return. In this capacity you are the teacher and your employees are the pupils. Your store meeting becomes the classroom. There are almost as many ideas on when, where, and how to hold a store meeting as there are merchants. My personal ideas are:

1. There should be at least one meeting per week, preferably on the same day.
2. All salespeople should see new merchandise as it comes in and familiarize themselves with it. At the store meeting have samples of merchandise you plan to discuss. Your salespeople

should be told at this time any history relevant to the item that you learned at the time of purchase. *You, as the buyer, should have a complete knowledge of your stock.* As with selling your customer, do not overwhelm your salespeople with too much information or you will confuse them.

3. Feature *"hot"* numbers as well as newly arrived goods. To further extend the effectiveness of this phase of your store meeting, use these same items to highlight your floor, and, when feasible, tie them into your windows. This can assure you of getting the most out of an item.

4. Remember, salespeople will take the course of least resistance in showing merchandise. If you feature certain goods at your store meetings, they will automatically push these goods. If you take the same item and tie it all together with T-stands, floor racks, and windows, it now becomes another selling tool which can result in multiple sales.

Selling is done in places other than your store. In Chapter 10, we discussed word-of-mouth advertising. Since advertising is a selling aid, let us examine how this particular form applies to you and your salespeople.

You come into contact with many people as you go through an average day—in the coffee shop, beauty parlor, barber shop, grocery store, post office, etc. Each of these people is a potential customer and should be told of your store. Special events, such as sales, are always of interest and should be talked up. This must be done in an unobtrusive manner, of course; and never forget that your most important selling tool is a pleasant disposition and a smile. If people like you, they will buy from you.

Nonselling Help

Nonselling help sets the tone of your business as much as the salesperson on your floor. Many of the above rules for selling help apply to cashiers, maids, and alteration people as

well. Their pleasant smile can do much to make the
customer's visit to your store as agreeable as possible. By the
time the customer has spent time with the salesperson shopping, trying on, fitting, and getting dressed again, he or she is
usually tired and in a hurry. The final steps in the purchase
should be handled as quickly as possible, with as little fuss as
your system permits.

A cashier is an important selling adjunct. This is an excel-
lent area for suggestive selling. Your cashier either can suggest simple accessories to go with the garment purchased (e.g.
a shirt and tie to go with a suit; a slip to go with a dress; hose)
or a completely different garment. "Have you looked at our
coats? We are running a pre-season sale." To encourage this
participation in the selling drive of the store by the cashier, I
would insist that the salesperson who had failed to suggest the
item be required to pay a "spiff," or small commission, to the
cashier. (This is only fair since that salesperson would not
have made the sale if the cashier had not been on the ball and
suggested that the customer take time to look.) In the case
where the cashier added to the sale by suggesting the right
accessories and sold the item herself, the cashier's portion of
the sale should be written up in a *"house"* book and the salesperson not credited for the additional merchandise, but only for
what he or she sold. This served two purposes: (1) it kept the
salespeople on their toes about suggesting additional goods,
and (2) it instilled some competition in the selling area.

This business of *"cash stand selling"* is considered so
important in some stores that certain "pick-up" items are
actually kept at the cash stand, such as hose, socks, ties, and
scarfs. These are items your customer may need but may
have forgotten, and the mere suggestion by the cashier can
mean an additional sale. Equally important, the customer
will appreciate being reminded of something she has forgotten, and you may have saved her another trip to the store. Of
course, another trip to the store isn't altogether bad—if it's

your store; but then you cannot be sure the customer will not go to a competitor.

Your cashier becomes important in still another way, for he or she is more than just a money-taker. The cashier is usually the last person to wait on the customer—or, to put it another way, the cashier is the store's *final impression* on that shopper. In show business, there is an old axiom: always leave them laughing. If not laughing, you should at least always leave them smiling, and that smile should come from a feeling of contentment with their purchase and contentment with your store.

Alteration people, more than maids, come into direct contact with the customer. They must project professionalism, confidence in their ability, and a pleasant disposition. A good tailor or alteration person can do much to close the sale and bring the customer back to the store. I have seen a good alteration person close a relatively weak sale for a salesperson simply because she showed the customer that, with a slight alteration, the garment would look beautiful. An alteration person must be able to communicate; it takes more than merely running a sewing machine, so keep this in mind when interviewing.

Before leaving this area of customer contact, there is one point which is often overlooked. Whoever answers the phone should be trained to do so correctly. The word *hello* should never be used alone; rather, *it must always be followed by the name of the store.* Depending on the time of year, the greeting should be "Merry Christmas, this is the ——— shop," or "Have a Happy Easter, this is the ——— shop," or "Happy Mother's Day (Father's Day), this is the ——— shop," or just, "Hello, this is the ——— shop." All of these not only identify the store but remind the caller of a particular reason for buying and hence become another selling tool.

One of my pet peeves is the hold button. I don't care if they

do play me pretty music while I am left hanging; hanging is
still hanging, and nothing can make it really pleasant. Never
let a customer hang too long waiting to have the call completed. This is bad image and is easily avoided by proper
training and instruction of everyone who may answer the
phone. If it is a question that will require some time to find the
answer, then take the customer's number and call him or her
back.

Delegating Responsibility in Your Store

In every store there can be only one boss, one person with
the final word. However, there must be a recognized second-
in-command. One of the most common reasons for disrup-
tion of a smooth operation is the inability of the manager to
retain active control either through illness or death. In this
situation there must be someone to assume the managerial
role and continue running the store.

If you, as the boss, fail to adequately train someone to fill
in for you and take charge, you will be adding another hazard
to the health of your business.

No boss is on the job every minute of every working day.
You will take an occasional day off or a vacation, or you will
be out of the store for markets or some personal matter. Yet
even in these times of absence, you must remain in control.
To maintain this absolute authority, here are a few simple
rules to keep in mind:

1. If you must be out of the store, appoint someone to act in
   your place on matters affecting decisions of daily store management. Make sure other employees know who this person
   is and the scope of his or here authority. Let it also be quite
   clear to everyone that this person is not *you*, merely a tem-
   porary replacement.
2. When you must be out of the store, even briefly, make sure

your assistant knows where to find you and when to expect you back. This applies to short absences such as, "I'm going to Joe's for lunch now, be back in 30 minutes." In one sentence you said you were leaving, where you were going, and when you could be expected to return. You should also let it be known that if something really important comes up, you are to be contacted. I used to say, "I am going to Joe's for lunch, be back in 30 minutes; call me only if the world comes to an end."

3. Never allocate duties which belong solely to you. Examples: signing checks, creating bank loans, dealing with creditors, hiring help. Since matters like charges, petty cash, inventory receiving, and the handing over of merchandise to buying customers are usually delegated duties, it would be wise to have regular audits by your accountant as a means of supervision and a precaution against fraud and theft.

4. Run service and honesty checks on your employees from time to time. For years we used a "shopper" service. They would come into the store as shoppers and make a purchase. As the owner, I did not even know when they would make a store visit. Afterwards, I would receive a written report on how they were greeted, the type of service received, how the sales slip was handled (whether the money went into the cash drawer or their pocket), whether suggestive selling was used, and what their final impression of the person waiting on them was. As a small-store operator, you may not wish the added expense of this type of service. It can be had at no cost if you have a friend do it for you. Of course, this friend must be someone your employees do not know.

5. Do not absent yourself from the store for too long a period at a time. A watched pot may never boil, but at least a watched pot will not boil over and make a mess of everything. Since you have all your eggs in this pot, watch it closely!

6. As we have noted elsewhere, it is always easier to hire someone than to fire someone. This authority to fire confirms that you are the boss. Just as you should never point a gun unless you are prepared to shoot, do not use this weapon as a threat.

If someone, because of dishonesty or total lack of ability is not performing to your expectations, dismissal is likely to be necessary. No one said being the boss was easy.

7. Money! Like my father used to say, "He who controls the allowance, controls!" Whoever signs the paychecks exercises absolute control. This is something that employees do not need to be constantly reminded of; rather, it is a self-evident fact of life.

Customer Buying: Charge Accounts

Most stores offer the customer three ways to buy: charge, cash, and layaway. Each of these ways is important to your customer's convenience and to your profits. Let's first examine charge accounts.

Let us assume, for the moment, that you do not "carry your own paper" (handle your own charges). What this leaves is the national and bank charges, MasterCard, Visa, Diners Club, American Express, and Carte Blanche. As a small store, you will not honor all of these cards. The customer will probably have at least two of the above and by some investigation (your banker is a good person to ask) you will know which are the two most important in your town. These then become the two you honor.

When you look into the world of "plastics," you will find more than one bank offering the same credit card. It is at this point that you begin to shop for the best deal you can make on the rate that you will be charged. Don't for a moment think that all charge the same service fee or that deals cannot be made. The differences between, for example, two banks offering the same credit card can vary from 1 to 1.5 percent and more. The rate is usually determined by the size of your account or—in the case of a new store just opening—by who wants your business the most. Their payment to you can run from *at once* to *too long*.

Another consideration will be what cards your competition is offering. Here again, look at stores nearly your own size. Department stores usually offer none of the national and bank charges but rather carry their own charges. You need offer no more than do the other stores of your size in your area.

If you wish to offer your own charge accounts, my advice, based on personal experience, is *don't!* Darryl Royal, the former great football coach of the University of Texas Longhorns, when asked by a sportswriter why his team seldom threw a pass, said, "When you put the ball in the air, three things can happen, and two of them are bad." I feel that offering your own charges is like throwing a pass—the bad reasons so outnumber the good that you might as well not try it.

Just because good 'ole Darryl and I say that something is wrong, doesn't mean it's necessarily so. Let me tell you why I think you should not carry your own paper (charge accounts). The handling of these charges requires a good deal of additional capital plus more help and many more expenses. You must establish your own credit department. This can run from one extra person to as many as it will take to process and collect your accounts. You have to have someone to approve credit, set credit limits, send statements and dunning mail, and—last but not least—call delinquent accounts. A *P&L account* (one charged off to *Profit and Loss* as uncollectable) is a direct charge to profits, as is the expense of collection.

The major hazard of "doing your own thing" here is the temptation to let so-called "good" customers overcharge on their account. It is an absolute must to be tough, and yet so difficult. At least when the bank says *no*, it's *no*, and you don't have to feel bad about turning down Mrs. Jones. Also, let us not forget the new government regulations with reference to the credit business. When these laws were written, they were not written by people who ever had to open and then collect a bad account! It's true, over the years there has been some abuse of customers when trying to collect, but every person who ever considered "beating" a bill may have celebrated when these new restrictions were placed on the business community.

Besides all of the above, you, as a new store owner, presumably just don't know enough about extending credit even to get involved. There are merchants who have been at it for 20 to 30 years who are still babes in the woods and are getting killed in their credit departments. The sad part about it is that they don't even know that they are getting killed by customers who understand the new credit laws better than they. So, after all of the above, if you have the capital and wish to offer in-house charge accounts, then I would be derelict in my duty if I didn't give you the primary rules of conduct.

Pay Plan

The quicker they pay up their account the more they can buy. The ideal situation is a 30-day charge. Today most stores offer a revolving charge, which calls for one tenth of the balance to be paid monthly. The service (or "carrying") charge on this type of account is 1.75 percent of the unpaid balance per month, or a maximum charge of 20 percent per year.

When offering any charge plan, there are certain *musts* to follow in order to have the best advantage (and hopefully hold your losses to a minimum). Investigate thoroughly, and pick those people to whom you wish to extend credit, as if they were diamonds. Limit the size balance you will permit each customer to maintain, and be sure that the customer fully understands the terms of payment. Follow up each account with a rapid and systematic collection program. If possible, delegate the responsibility of implementing your credit—extending and collecting—to one person. Make

absolutely certain that everyone working in the store understands all policies pertaining to credit.

In addition to 30-day accounts and revolving accounts,
there is one more used in smaller stores that permits the customer to make a single large purchase (e.g. a fur) and have a
longer time to pay up. This is done on a separate account,
rather than putting it on the customer's revolving account, so
that they do not go way over the limit set and so become
unable to buy anything else from you for an extended period.

The most serious problem that you will face as a small merchant granting credit derives from your need to be both sales-
and credit-oriented. Both are specializations. The amount of
business you do may not justify the hiring of a full-time person who is familiar with the granting and collection of
accounts. As your own credit manager, you are already busy
with all the other duties of management, such as buying and
selling. The person who is sales-oriented should not as a rule
have the responsibility of granting credit. As the store owner,
you should be *sales*-minded, and the temptation to over-
extend a balance to complete a sale can be too great.

I spoke of establishing a sound credit policy and then
adhering to it and making everyone in the store aware of that
policy. There are four fundamental types of policy:

1. *Easy credit and an easy-collection follow-up.* Under this system, you are going after big sales and hoping that your
   volume covers your losses; therefore, forget everything I told
   you about markup and plan to use a much greater percentage. If you decide to offer credit, you will eventually have
   "bad debts" and you will need this "cover." When we speak of
   "easy collection" follow-up, it means sending only a monthly
   statement showing the amount past due and a "friendly"
   reminder to pay.

2. *Easy credit and hard collection work.* This could be called
   "my faith in myself as a collector of bad debts." You are once
   again looking for the larger sales volume with confidence that

you will be able to collect. Hard collection methods would include a speeding-up of collection notices, a more severe message, telephone calls, and, as a last resort, legal action (where applicable).

3. *A tough credit-granting policy followed by an easy collection system.* Here you eliminate the fringe-type accounts (accounts which you might decline, based on past paying habits to other stores), and try not to hurt anyone's feelings by being too harsh in trying to collect.

4. Last, and what I think best for the new merchant, is *tough credit-granting followed by hard collection* procedures (as described in (2) above). Under this system, you are hopefully selling only good accounts and keeping your risk to a minimum.

Follow-Up

In the days before every store offered charge accounts, those that did stuck to plan (4) above. There were a great many customers who could not get credit at a regular store, so they were forced to buy in stores specializing in this service. These stores were called "credit stores" and differed from so-called "regular stores" in their markup and collection policy, or follow-up.

I am assuming that you are going to open a "regular fashion store" and that your policy fill fall between (3) and (4) above. No matter what you do, you must work out some sort of system to follow up not only on accounts that miss payment but on those that make substandard payments. If a cashier receives a payment for less than the agreed-upon terms, it should be mentioned to the customer. If the payment comes through the mail, then a thank-you note along with noting the substandard amount should be sent to the customer when you mail the receipt. If two payments in a row are below the agreed amount, the cashier should call in the credit manager (or you) either to make new arrangements or at least to discuss the problem with the customer. This is a very delicate area and requires a diplomatic touch.

It should go without saying that the "turn" in receivables is just as important as the "turn" in merchandise. *If you do not collect the money owed you, you are, in reality, giving the goods away.* A slow turn in receivables indicates that credit limits are being set too high for the customer and that the customer cannot pay according to the terms. Limits must be set realistically. The two-fold risk that you run in overselling a customer is that customers who are overextended may stop paying you and at the same time keep up an account elsewhere so that they can buy *somewhere.* You then lose both the money owed you and future business as well.

New Accounts

New accounts are the lifeblood of a charge operation. If you decide that this is the way you want to go, then make a concentrated effort to secure new charge customers. Just as you talk up your store to everyone with whom you come in contact, talk up charge accounts. You can even offer incentives to your salespeople and cashier to open new accounts.

Now comes the important part of the whole credit operation. The customer has been convinced (and this is not too difficult) that he or she should have an account in your store. Your first step is the *Credit Application. Above all, make sure that your application form meets all the new consumer government regulations.* It is best to have this form checked by an attorney.

Segal Rule on credit applications: You are exchanging merchandise for this piece of paper from which to collect money. If you do not have enough (or correct) information, you will have nothing to trace down anyone who *skips.* The application must contain this basic information: *correct name, correct address, ability to pay, can the customer be made to (judgment proof or not)*, plus any other information the *law allows.*

After the application is completed, it must be verified and a credit report drawn. This can be done by calling the local Retail Credit Bureau. By doing this, you establish two things: whether you want to open the account at all, and what line (amount) of credit to use. When a customer comes in who has not used his or her account in several months, reverify the information on the application. If the customer has a good record-of-payment previously, it is not necessary to draw another report, unless in talking to the customer you feel that it is a good idea.

Credit: Pros and Cons

Books have been written on credit and collections. I have merely attempted to highlight the subject and the avenues to follow if you wish to embark on this phase of the business. To repeat what was at the beginning of this section, I do not advise going this route unless you have lots of money and a complete understanding of how credit works. To sum it all up, let me give you the advantages and disadvantages of extending credit.

Advantages of extending credit: It is easier to make sales; people have a tendency not to be concerned about the price if they are charging; they buy more and therefore increase the volume; they are *your* customers; they tend to buy better goods; the customer buys things he could not afford to buy if he had to pay cash; and it is convenient for the customer.

Disadvantages of extending credit: It ties up working capital; it increases your cost of operation; it can force you to borrow money and thereby cost you the additional expense of the interest on the money; it can lull both you and the customer into a sense of false security about their ability to pay;

charge customers may return more goods because they have not paid for them (and what are you going to do with a person who owes you a large balance?); it raises your markup and could make you less competitive with other stores; and the refusal of an additional charge to an already established account can cause ill-will and put the collection of the balance in jeopardy.

Testing Your System

Let us assume that you are extending credit to those of your customers whom you think are honest and able to pay their bills. There is a simple form that you can use to judge just how right (or wrong) you have been in your granting of credit. This step taken by your credit person (or by you) is known as "aging your accounts." It is done on a form known as an *accounts receivable age analysis.*

Take a five-column sheet and head the columns: *Balance, Current, 30-day, 60-day, 90-day,* and *over 90* respectively (see p. 166). These headings refer to the condition (or age) of the account at the time of the "aging." Some stores age their accounts every month, others use a longer period of time between agings. Since this is such a vital part of business, and since you will not be running a great many charge accounts, I would suggest that you use the monthly system.

As we said earlier, there are two types of charge accounts —*30-day* and *revolving.* This should be noted on the customer's account ledger; it will guide you to the proper column for recording the customer's balance on the aging. Total balance of each account, regardless of its condition, is recorded first in the column headed *Balance.* If a payment was made in the previous month, record the balance again under the column headed *Current.*

Example: if you are "aging" on September 1st, any purchase or payment made in August would be current. If the

Accounts Receivable Age Analysis Sheet

Age Analysis
May 31, 19——

A/c # (if any)	Name	Balance		Current (May)		30-day (April)		60-day (March)		90-day or older (February-Back)	
1	Alagna	80	30	80	30						
2	Andrews	46	—			46	—				
3	Bagelman	33	—	33	—						
4	Bierbrier	24	50	24	50						
5	Carter	101	10					101	10		
6	Chaiken	63	—	63	—						
7	Dexter	49	95	49	95						
8	Feldman	52	—	52	—						
9	Gallop	81	—			81	—				
10	Golman	77	—	77	—						
11	Gross	26	50	26	50						
12	Heath	39	99	39	99						
13	Hopkins	41	60	41	60						
14	Jones	28	70			28	70				
15	King	42	22	42	22						
16	Miller	16	10	16	10						
17	Morris	19	95					19	95		
18	Norton	36	70							36	70
19	Olsen	42	44	42	44						
20	Rubin	53	80	53	80						
21	Schumann	55	—	55	—						
22	Smith	33	20					33	20		
23	Stewart	115	—	115	—						
24	Turner	90	—	90	—						
25	Tycher	80	—	80	—						
26	Unger	10	15							10	15
27	Weber	32	80	32	80						
28	White	51	40	51	40						
	Total	1 423	40	1 066	60	155	70	154	25	46	85
	%			74	93	10	93	10	83	3	29

last payment was made in July, you would then record it in the column marked *30-day*; if made in June, it would then be recorded as *60-day*; and so on.

After you have recorded every account on your books, total each column. The balance column will tell you exactly how much you have outstanding in accounts receivable. The total of the other columns will give you the percentage of each step on the ladder of delinquency. See—I told you it was simple.

Once you have determined which accounts will never be collected, (and there may well be some), they should be *"charged off"* your books. This is an accounting procedure that your accountant will handle for you.

Other bookkeeping procedures are you *Sales and Cash Receipts Journal*, the *Daily Summary*, the *Accounts Receivable Ledger*, and the *Cash Disbursements, Purchases, and Expense Journal*. I only mention these procedures since your accountant will no doubt suggest that you keep them. In many cases the accountant himself will do the posting and maintain these books or show you how to accumulate the information to be recorded.

For the most part the names of the journals are self-explanatory (we retailers try not to get too complicated). A *Sales and Cash Receipts Journal* is the book wherein you record all income *cash* and your sales; *The Daily Summary* is a recap of each day's income and outgo; the *Accounts Receivable Ledger* is the record of all money owed the business, from whatever source; and the *Cash Disbursements, Purchases, and Expense Journal* basically is the opposite of the *Receivable Ledger*, showing what is going out.

Although your accountant will show you how to set up these various ledgers or may even keep them himself it's important to understand thoroughly what they are and how they function.

Customer Buying: Layaway

Layaway means exactly what it says: you are taking an item out of your stock and laying it away to be picked up at a later date by the customer. When you do this, you are reducing the inventory that you have to show other customers, with no guarantee that the item laid away will ever be picked up.

Many smaller stores are discontinuing this service because of the cost factor. However, if you intend to offer layaways, much of what has been said pertaining to charge accounts holds true here as well. Finally, there are some rules that apply exclusively to layaways and that should be adhered to:

1. Limit the items to be put into layaway to major garments or items where the amount of the sale justifies the service.
2. Obtain the largest possible deposit to better ensure your chance that the item will be picked up when the time comes.
3. Merchandise held in layaway too long becomes a markdown when it is returned to stock because of nonpayment. Example: a white dress put into layaway in June and returned to stock in August goes directly onto the sale rack and usually at half price.
4. Deposits and payments belong to you (depending on state laws where you operate) in the event of a return to stock for nonpayment. The rule that I followed in my operation was to put the money in a forfeiture account, and if the customer selected another garment of like value, I would give credit from the amount paid on the previous layaway. I also tried to hold the customer to the same department, but this rule was often bent (if not broken). Under no circumstances would I permit a cash refund or the layaway money to be applied to a charge balance. This is not an unfair practice, since you have tied up your merchandise for the customer and the money paid in often does not cover the expenses you incurred from trying to collect and from the markdowns you were forced to take. In no case would I permit a second garment to go into

layaway using the credit from a *return* as the deposit. A substantial new deposit would have to be made. Keep in mind, the only "hold" you have on the customer, crudely stated, is the amount of money the customer stands to lose if he or she reneges on the agreement. Depending on the circumstances, I rarely gave credit for money paid after a second "pull" (return to stock).

Customer Buying: Cash Sales, Discounts

Cash sales are the most desirable way of doing business; the subject really needs no explanation, but it is here that we can touch on *discounts.* Some stores make it a practice to give discounts on cash purchases or to relatives and friends. Giving a discount because someone pays cash is not a good practice on the face of it. Customers may look at you and your store and think you are making a great deal of money. They do not have the knowledge of business to know that you work hard and the return on your investment is tied to many economic factors, and they may think that a discount for cash means that you have a long markup to enable you to afford the discount. So it is best to avoid this trap.

Friends' and relatives' discounts are another story, and this is a tricky area. Good friends and understanding relatives will not ask for a discount when you *first* go into business. They will shop with you out of a feeling of wanting to help you get established and not consider you only as a *wholesale resource.* However, as ideal as this would be, you may still be asked. So how to set limits, not offend, and keep within a store policy becomes the question.

A major department store in my town became so involved in giving discounts that they had to prepare a book for each cash stand throughout the store listing who was entitled to a discount and the amount. The discounts ran from 10 percent for friends up to 40 percent for immediate family of the owners and those very close to the owners.

If you have a friend in another type of business who gives you a discount, the reciprocating becomes a sort of trade-off. This is a two-way deal and is good for both of you. Your immediate family (and I mean immediate) will rightly expect, and you will give, a discount. And there will be that closest friend (who is like immediate family) to whom you will want to give a discount—so give it. It has been said that "No law was ever written which couldn't be broken"; just make sure that when you break your "discount law," you do it with good reason.

I have only touched on the highlights of selling. It is conceivable that entire volumes could be written on each section of this chapter. If I can leave you with but one thought, it would be: your store should be run by happy, pleasant, and smiling people; your customer should be made to feel welcome and have sufficient inventory from which to choose; and your merchandise and atmosphere should project the image you want while filling your store's niche in the business community.

Twelve

Storekeeping

Even a pretty face has to be washed.

Housekeeping Your Store

At this point let us take a look at the store and why it is a place where, all other things being equal, your customer will want to shop. The message is **Keep It Clean!** These words cover a multitude of areas and require constant attention. Let us begin at the front door and work our way through the store.

1. Keep the front well swept and the windows washed. If your store has a recessed alcove at the front door, you should never permit trash to accumulate. I have never seen this type of front that didn't look messy every morning from the wind blowing in all manner of things. Therefore, your first job *every* morning should be to sweep. And this may need to be repeated during the day if necessary. No matter how beautifully you have trimmed the windows, a dirty alcove will detract.

This detraction holds true for dirty windows. If the customer has to look through dirty glass to see your display, nothing can look the way you want it to look. Window washing is not a daily task. Twice a week will usually be enough under normal circumstances. This job is usually done by a window washing service and not by the store people. As with any other expense item, shop for price.

2. Vacuum the carpet every morning.

3. A tile floor should be mopped at least once a week. This should always be done at night. A wet floor is dangerous during the day and invites lawsuits should customers slip and injure themselves. To some people suing is a way of life—so be careful! The mopping can be done by the window washing service.

4. The way you keep your stock could very easily cover an entire chapter. This problem requires constant attention, and I say *problem* simply because it is one of the most overlooked jobs in the store. Merchandise must be properly in stock. *Properly* means the right type of hangers for a particular garment, buttons buttoned (womenswear only), nothing hanging on spindles outside the bins, sizes in their proper place, colors hung together, etc.

5. Since it is self-evident that merchandise cannot sell in the receiving room, it become a *never-to-be-broken* rule that goods just in from the manufacturer get ticketed, hung on the proper hangers, and put into stock as quickly as possible. Do not let merchandise hang on hooks around the store waiting to be put away. If they are badly wrinkled, they should be steamed out before they go into stock. One badly wrinkled garment can make your whole stock look shabby.

Everyone Should Do His/Her Bit

Have you ever walked into a store and admired how neat and clean the stock appeared and wondered why it was a more desirable place to shop than the store you just left? The primary reason for this difference is the attitude of the people working in the store.

Let me relate a personal experience to illustrate this point: Several years ago I paid a visit to one of my stores and arrived at about eleven in the morning. At this point the store had been open for business for about an hour and a half. The vestibule was littered with trash that had blown in during the night. I asked my manager why it had not been swept out and was told, "The maid was sick and had called to say she wouldn't be in at all." Answers such as this have a very bad effect on a boss's blood pressure. I walked straight back to the utility closet, took a broom, and swept out the front. It may have been beneath my manager's dignity to push a broom, but I was only the president of the firm and it wasn't beneath mine. Needless to say, because of this attitude (which carried over into other areas of that manager's responsibilities) the manager did not stay on our team.

This attitude of "everyone does his bit" should hold true in your store. There is no room in a small store for *prima donna* salespeople, even if they are good. As their leader, it is your responsibility to see that they pull their just share of the load.

This does not mean that good salespeople will not get, and deserve, more privileges than poor salespeople. They earn this *right* by virtue of their worth to the overall operation of your business.

Each salesperson should be assigned a department of his or her own to keep straight. It should be that person's job first thing every morning to do whatever is necessary to make that area presentable. If it takes a little effort to use some Windex on the mirrors or to run a vacuum cleaner, so be it! Neither job is beneath anyone's dignity.

Mopping and scrubbing vestibules and washing windows, as I have said, should be done by a paid service. There are cleaning companies listed in the Yellow Pages, and these will give you bids by the size of your store and the number of windows involved. This expense, like all others, should be shopped for by price, and you should select the one that best serves your purpose and is within your budget. This does not include sweeping the front, since you should not have to hire anyone to do that for you.

Lights are important and are far more than mere illumination. They create moods, help your image, and generally round out the picture you present to the customer. Develop the habit of looking up at the ceiling and glancing around at the bins whenever you walk into the store, checking for burned-out bulbs. There is nothing more detracting than a dark area that should be lighted. It can make the entire store look unkempt.

If you and your salespeople remember that the store is your home away from home, the task of keeping it clean will be made a lot easier. You spend more waking hours each day in your store than you do in your home. Realizing this it should be evident that the store can be no less clean than your house. What some of your people may tolerate in their own homes may not be good enough for the store. Consider each customer as a guest in your home, and prepare the "house" for company every day.

Receiving Room, Rest Room and Stock Room

The Receiving Room

All stores, no matter how large or small, must have someplace to receive, ticket, and prepare incoming merchandise for the selling floor. This space is called the receiving room, and should (as with the cash stand) be kept to an efficient and workable minimum.

In a small store with a limited number of employees, everyone at one time or another will be required to work in the receiving room. Even though it is *in the back* and hidden from the customers, cleanliness is the cardinal rule. Neat working areas create efficient and happy employees and tend to reduce mistakes. Show me a messy desk and office and I will show you someone operating at a lower capacity for work and accuracy than he or she is capable of doing.

The physical set-up of the receiving room is obviously dependent on the size of the space you have allocated for this purpose. There are certain basic elements that compose a receiving room, and space to house them is essential:

1. A desk: used to keep order copies and a place to write.
2. Shelves: used to keep supplies (i.e. size tickets, sale tags, sealing tape, etc.).
3. Hang rod: to hang incoming merchandise while you check it against the order copy and change to proper hangers.
4. Storage boxes: for storing and sorting hangers.
5. Trash bin.

When the freight truck pulls up to your back door to deliver the goods that you bought at market, there is set into motion a series of events known as *receiving procedures*. What these procedures are—and how they affect your profits—is a matter of great importance.

Let us start with fundamentals: First of all, make sure that the package or box is addressed to *your* store. This may sound simplistic but, as I said, let us be fundamental.

Let's stay simple—open the box and hang up the merchandise. Today, most manufacturers ship *on hangers*. What this means is that the factory packs the goods on wire or cheap plastic hangers and covers each garment with lightweight plastic bags. Remove the bags and place the empties in a trash container. The reason for this is that plastic bags lying on the floor are like ice on a sidewalk—*slippery!* This hint will be appreciated by your insurance agent.

After you have hung up the goods (on racks provided for this purpose when you built the receiving room), it is time to *check in the shipment*.

Checking

Checking in a shipment and *checking off the order copy* mean the same thing. When you went to market (or the salesperson came to your store) and you purchased merchandise, you wrote an order. A copy of that order remains with you and should be filed alphabetically in your receiving room.

In checking off the order copy, there are definite steps to follow:

1. Check your completion date on the order. If the style numbers you have just received are within the allotted time, then you keep the merchandise. If the goods are *past due*, then you have to make a decision. If you need this particular type of goods, you should keep it; but if you do not need it, return it to the manufacturer. *This is your option.*

2. Assuming that you are keeping the styles received, your next step is to change hangers. Various types of hangers (skirt, short-neck plastic, long-neck plastic, etc.) should be sorted by type. Some stores use special floor racks made for this purpose, some use old cardboard boxes, some have a wall rack and hang their hangers by type; but whatever system you use, keep your hangers handy and separated by type.

   It is in your receiving room that all merchandise should be put on the correct hangers before they reach your stock. During the course of the day, hangers can get mixed up (either by the customers or by lazy employees) but this is no excuse for their staying that way.

   Train your salespeople to be constantly on the alert for mixed-up hangers: when they see a garment on the wrong hanger, they should change it *immediately*. This takes only a minute and keeps your store looking as if it were run by professionals.

3. Once you have changed the hangers, check off the order copy. This simply means circling the sizes and colors ordered and received. If you ordered a dress in blue, one each in sizes 8, 12, 16, and in green one each in sizes 10 and 14, for a total of five pieces, make sure that that is what you received.

4. Once you are satisfied that the merchandise has been received as ordered, you should inspect every garment for obvious flaws. Any reputable manufacturer inspects his own goods before shipping, but remember, we are dealing with the human element, and sometimes a damaged garment slips through. As I have said before: if it is a simple flaw that you can fix easily, *fix it*; do not return it to the vendor. If it is serious damage, you are within your rights to return it, and you should.

5. Your next step is called *ticketing*. This means printing (either by hand or by machine) the information you desire for bookkeeping purposes. This should include numerical codes indicating department (e.g., blouses, pants, dresses, suits, coats), manufacturer, style number, color, and price. You will note I did not say *size*. Some stores print the size on the ticket. I prefer colored tickets to indicate size. See chart page 178.

   The reasons that I used a color code were: (*a*) Our salespeople could see at a glance if a garment was hanging in the wrong spot. By just making sure that all of the same color tickets were hanging together, we kept our stock straight with the least effort. (*b*) It became a selling aid. For example, a customer might come in and say that she wears a size 14—yet one look at her and it is obvious she needs a size 16. Without deceiving your customer, you could simply say, "All of the blue tickets are your size." The customer was probably fitted correctly for the first time, and she is happy with the store. It also works well for the customer who knows her correct size. She knows that anywhere in the store, if a garment has a certain color ticket, it will fit her. This saves a lot of looking at tickets by the shopper and the salesperson.

6. There is but one step left before putting the merchandise in stock, and that is pressing. Not every garment coming in

needs pressing—only those that are badly wrinkled. To press them all would be a waste of time and effort. There are inexpensive steamers available for this purpose; every store should have a steamer not only for badly wrinkled incoming merchandise, but also for use in the alteration department, for garments going into or coming out of the windows, and for customer returns. A steamer is a necessary expense you really should consider.

APPAREL COLOR CODE CHART

	Sizes		
Ticket Color	Dresses, Coats, Sportswear, Robes	Sweaters Blouses, Swimwear	Menswear
Dark Green	3–4		
Dark Tan	5–6		
Light Tan	7–8		
White	S–9–10		Size
Pink	11–12	32	written on
Light Green	M–13–14–12½	34	ticket
Blue	15–16–14½	36	
Yellow	L–18–16½	38	
Red	20–18½	40	
Orange	42–20½	42	
Lilac	44–22½	44	
Grey	X-Large sizes with size written on ticket.		

The Rest Room

The required number of rest rooms in a store is usually controlled by local ordinances which are set forth in the municipal building codes. The number is usually based on the square footage of your store. The main thing to remember is: *keep it clean*. An ill-kept restroom destroys any image your windows or interior design otherwise make.

As I have said repeatedly, *a customer entering your store is like a guest in your home.* If you would be embarrassed by an unclean bathroom at home, then you should be equally embarrassed by a similar condition in your store.

Using this comparison, the restroom now becomes the guestroom. As such, decorate it the same way you would any other part of the store. Little touches, such as a box of facial tissues in a holder, pictures (preferably miniatures), or a pretty soap dish are not out of the ordinary.

But above all your restroom must be clean.

The Stock Room

This is the name generally given to that area of the store where reserve stock is kept. *Storage* or *out-of-season* merchandise should be held to almost nothing. *You can't sell goods in the stock room.* Incoming merchandise should be unpacked, ticketed, and put into stock as quickly as possible. Fashion is a fragile thing at best, so do not cut into your selling time.

There will be occasions when it is necessary to retain certain merchandise out-of-stock in a stock room. Duplicate sizes or colors and out-of-season goods are but two examples. When this occurs, your reserve stock should be arranged in such a manner as to keep it neat, clean, and easily accessible.

If it is hanging goods (e.g., dresses, blouses, sport shirts, etc.) it may be a good idea to cover them with a sheet to prevent dust from settling on the shoulders and to keep the lights from fading the colors along the hanger line. Boxed goods (e.g. bras, socks, hose, etc.) should be arranged by size and color to facilitate finding them quickly for a customer.

The stock room should be checked daily against your out-front stock, and your reserve stock should be blended into your inventory as fast as possible. Never have anything in your stock room which is out of reach of the customer.

Out-of-season merchandise should be reviewed periodically for its quickest return to the active inventory. Be sure to reticket before returning it to stock. Some can be marked back up to regular price while others may be used on a preseason sale rack.

Never lose sight of the fact that storekeeping is a function of everyone working in the store. It has been said that people are judged by how they dress; if so, then it holds true that a store is also judged by its appearance.

Thirteen

Record Keeping

*Ships keep logs to know
where they have been...
stores to know where they are going!*

There are records and there are records, and each is kept
for a different reason. Some records you keep merely because
you wish to (curiosity), some because they are necessary to
the operation of your business (expenses and merchandising),
and some because you *must* (the government).

In this time of inflation, heavy taxation, and multiple government regulations—to say nothing of competing with the
store next door—every business must keep records if it ex-
pects to succeed. You will find it imperative to keep records
that accurately paint a complete picture of purchasing, sales,
inventory, depreciation, payroll, credit, collections, personnel, expenses, and anything else required by law or common
sense to operate your business. Properly kept records become
the hands that remove the store-owner's blindfold and permit
a clear view toward the future.

What records you keep will greatly depend on what information you need. Not all merchants want the same type and quantity of data. The type and size of the business you intend to operate will dictate how many and what kind of records you will keep. Just be careful. There are many shortcuts to inefficiency.

In the creation of a record-keeping system, there are certain considerations of which you must never lose sight:

1. It should be as uncomplicated as possible, while giving you all the data you need.
2. It must be as current as possible if you are to derive any benefit from it as a daily reference and guide.
3. It should not unnecessarily duplicate data, since every time you create a record that essentially gives you the same information that you have elsewhere, this becomes an added expense.
4. It must be correct. To achieve this degree of accuracy, your system must contain a series of checks and balances.

Even though it is important to be in contact with your customers, it is equally vital that you allot sufficient time to the study and interpretation of the *"numbers."* It is by these numbers that your business rises or falls. If this sounds contradictory—it's not.

As we discussed at some length in our chapter on expenses, it is this factor that decides profit and loss. Through the proper use of your records, you can exercise control. I would suggest using your accountant the way he or she was meant to be used. While you are learning—and the process never really stops—have your accountant explain each and every item submitted. What is even more important, have the relationship between items set in their proper perspective. How can we understand why the utility bills are out of line if we do not understand when and how to use our lights and air conditioning?

1. They furnish a history of what has been and serve as a guide to the future by showing how you stand at present.

2. They help you give Uncle Sam his just due by reflecting a true profit or loss picture of your business.
3. They enable you to supply information to the proper credit agencies on which your line of credit can be established.
4. They serve as a safety valve to keep and protect the profits and assets of your business.
5. They can be a source base for exchanging information with your suppliers and competitors when the need arises.

No matter what type of business format you decide to use —corporation, partnership, or proprietorship—you will be required to keep records supplying the Internal Revenue Service with certain information. Nowhere does the IRS firmly state what, and how many, records you as the taxpayer must maintain. The government assumes that all taxpayers will decide what records they should keep in order to determine their tax liability and to back up any and all statements made on their tax returns.

This should really cause you no problem, since you, as with most companies, will have a bookkeeping system geared to provide you with management information and financial data for reporting purposes. This will usually be much more than IRS requires. *Beware of the trap of oversimplification in your bookkeeping.* Some small firms, especially when first going into business, are guilty of this and find themselves paying additional taxes, interest, and penalties. In such cases, the government could file against you for negligence and fraud. This is highly unlikely, but you could lose legitimate tax deductions and credits or have to pay taxes that you could have legally deferred to another year if you had had proper records.

The Books You Will Keep

So now that you have been told not to keep too many records, but to be sure to keep enough records—what is *enough*? Let's look at some of them:

Company Checkbook: To make your life as simple as possible use only one checking account. Transact all your business through this one account, and have another account for your personal business. Do not commingle these monies. Reconcile your checkbook with the statement you receive from the bank *each* and *every* month.

Cash Receipts Journal: This needs almost no explanation; it is where you record all receipts—payments received, checks, miscellaneous receipts, etc.—in other words, money coming in.

Cash Disbursement Journal: Basically this is the opposite of the *Cash Receipts Journal.* It is in this record that you list all monies paid out by both cash and checks. As I said before, pay by check through one account wherever possible. If you have paid out cash (e.g. parking, business lunch, stamps), this must be accompanied by a petty-cash voucher.

Payroll Register or Journal: Federal payroll tax laws are uniform in the 50 states. In addition, there are varying degrees of state, county, and city taxes due, depending on where your business is located. It can run the gamut from New York City, where you must collect several different income taxes, to Texas which has no personal or corporate income taxes.

What the IRS Wants

The IRS does not require you to maintain your records in any specific format, but you must be able to provide them documentation including the following information:

Name, address, and Social Security number of everyone working for you.

The date, amount, and period of time involved for every salary payment made.

The exact amount of taxable income paid.

The exact amount of withholding tax withheld and the date.
Your employer identification number.

Here are some pointers to help you in keeping employee records:

1. Keep copies of all government forms you submit.
2. You will be required in most cases to make deposits of the amount of taxes withheld to a government depository (usually a large bank) quarterly. Keep a record of these amounts and the dates you make the deposits.
3. If you pay employees while they are off, keep track of their pay rate and the amount paid.
4. At the time you hire an employee, you are required to obtain a withholding exemption certificate. Keep this on file.
5. If an employee is not a citizen of the United States, keep any government forms relating to alien status.
6. If the employee is given anything (e.g.: merchandise, dinner) in lieu of salary, make sure it is recorded somewhere.

For Social Security (FICA) taxes, the following records should be kept:

The gross amount of the employee's salary used as a basis for determining FICA taxes.
The date and amount of FICA collected.

Before you conclude that the set of books created by the above IRS requirements would fill a library, let us consider how you will keep this information.

Set up a card or buy a payroll book that shows the following: (a) pay period, (b) hours worked, (c) earnings, (d) deductions and (e) net pay. This record will cover most of the requirements we have listed and is quite easy to keep. This book is inexpensive and can be purchased in any office supply store. I recommend the book, since it is bound and creates a permanent record.

Computers?

As a small-store operator, you may feel that computers and the many-splendored world of fancy bookkeeping are not for you. It is true that the computer systems used at U.S. Steel, General Motors, and Neiman Marcus, if applied to a small business, would be like killing a fly with a howitzer.

Increasingly, however, adaptations are being made by computer people that are conforming to the needs of smaller operations. As time progresses, they are more and more gearing themselves to the small business. You yourself may not have your own computer set-up but would instead use a *service*. These services can perform many functions such as producing operating statements, profit and loss statements, payroll records, general ledgers, accounts payable, etc., for a set fee per month. This fee may in many cases be less (and more accurate) than what the employees you might hire to do the same job would cost.

There again, as I have said over and over when discussing money to be spent for services or supplies, *shop around for price*; not all service companies charge the same rate for the same work. As a smaller store, your requirements can usually be handled by a standard program already set up for the computer. The biggest cost factor is the development of a program designed to your specifications. It is wise, therefore, for you to conform to an established system rather than have the computer people create a program specifically for you.

Do not be afraid to investigate the use of computers! We can't roll back the calendar, and the days of the stand-up desk and quill pens are gone. The way of the future will be computers; therefore, their use in a manner adjusted to the small business can prove most beneficial to you.

We spoke above about the use of a *computer service* to serve your bookkeeping needs. In our rapidly progressing world of data processing we have seen the evolution of the desk-top or *microcomputers*. This is not to be confused with the *minicomputers* which are larger and considerably more expensive. The microcomputer can be obtained for approximately $2500–5000, including the programs, as compared to about $25,000 for a minicomputer.

When shopping for a computer there are certain words in "computer language" with which you should be familiar. *Hardware* is the machine itself; *software* are the programs which make the machine do what you want; *time sharing* is when more than one company uses the same computer (usually through a computer service); *programs*, instructions in a language only understood by a computer to serve a certain function (same as software), and a *terminal*, a typewriter-like keyboard for letters, attached to a 10-key board for numbers, with which you enter your date and a *monitor* or *CRT display* for showing you what you have entered and displaying answers. These are just a few words out of a very large computer vocabulary.

A computer is not a magic machine which will automatically make you a successful merchant by merely pushing a button. It is a sophisticated piece of machinery geared to offer the small businessperson two distinct advantages—speed and accuracy. These are the same reasons which impelled big business to turn to computers in the first place. The fast turn in apparel, the need to have information today, not tomorrow, is pushing small business in the same direction.

The one thing that prevents more small entrepreneurs from taking advantage of this tool of modern business is *fear*. Fear of the unknown costs, of changing from their old ways, of admitting that they can improve on the current system, and the fear that comes from a lack of knowledge with regard to computers.

The microcomputer is geared to the small businessperson. It takes up a minimum amount of space (usually fits on the top of a desk), requires no operator, offers different software programs (e.g., payroll, accounting, inventory, etc.) on cassette tapes, and basically is a one-time expense, as compared to the monthly charge by a service bureau doing the same job.

There is no way that I can make you a computer expert in one chapter, or even in one book, but if you are curious enough your public library is full of just such books. To further your education in this area you can talk to hardware and software salespeople and attend seminars on this subject.

Computers, much more so than manual bookkeeping procedures, can lead you into the trap of *curiosity information*. This type of data has two pitfalls. First, it costs more. For each step the computer does for you, you pay! You should get only that information which you *must* have, and, as with supplies and merchandise, do not overbuy. Second, curiosity information requires time to read and digest. If you are a good merchant, you want to spend as little time as possible sitting at a desk (reading) and as much time as possible on your selling floor talking to, and waiting on customers.

Your Budget Record

Like a well-run household, your business must establish a budget and then use it to realize your goals. A budget is not chiseled in stone; it is a living, breathing part of your business and so is subject to change based on the many variables that form the basis of business.

Your budget should set forth a definite goal toward which you must strive. Goal-setting is an important phase of living, especially when planning a business operation.

The goals for a small business can take the form of desired sales, estimated expenses, place in the community, reputation and future expansion, to name a few. All of the above must be budgeted, in either time or money, and fit into your overall plan.

Your aim when dealing with any budgetary figures is to see how close you can come to staying within their guidelines and to maintain a proper balance between what's coming in and what's going out. A properly kept budget record will show you at a glance the variances between estimated expenses and actual expenses. These you must know, in order to make the proper adjustments as you go along. It is not good to look up one day and say, "Wow, how did I spend this much money?" and then have to make a choice between paying the light bill and running an ad. To put it more simply, a budget relegates each expense to its proper slot and by so doing prevents waste of funds; it sets financial policies by showing the effects of sales on your ability to raise money (cash flow); it is a roadmap to future expansion of your business by setting forth what and how much financing you will require. In the end, a budget helps formulate an adequate set of books, which in turn keeps you on your desired path.

You should use your budget to pinpoint weaknesses, divert monies into proper channels, control waste, establish priorities for spending, and determine future money needs.

Since your budget is a guide based on expected income and expenditures, all of the above becomes subject to revision and should be eyed with current trends in mind. After working out your budget, it should be apparent where the weaknesses are in your plans and operation. You may note overspending in one place and underspending in another. By diverting money from one to the other you can use your money more effectively. When looking at your budget "on paper," it should be easy to set your priorities and, by so doing, establish your immediate money needs.

Breaking Even

At all times a good merchant knows what it will take for him to "break even." Let us discuss how you determine at what point this happens. *Break even* means exactly what it says: you are not *making* money, but equally important, you are not *losing* money. Making this determination can be done easily: divide your monthly expenses by 26 (number of business days) to arrive at a daily expense. This should include such items as rent, salaries, utilities, telephone, plus calculated other expense (e.g. supplies and services). Once you have this figure, you determine your gross profit by reducing the gross sales by the maintained markup. If your prorated expenses are $300 per day, you must do at least $600 per day in sales ($600 in sales less a 50 percent markup leaves a $300 gross profit) to break even.

Knowing your break-even figure can be a guide for planning. Many variables come into play; sales volume, markup, fixed expenses, and controllable expenses interact to produce this break-even figure. As the owner, you should know if each day is carrying its share of the load. We used to call this, "How much does it cost us to turn the key each morning?" When you know this, you have your target zeroed in, and then you take your best shot to create the needed sales to show a profit.

<h2 style="text-align:center">Balance Sheet
and
Profit and Loss Statement</h2>

We have discussed the merchandising and budget reports, which are day-to-day means of bookkeeping. This now brings us to those statements that tell us if what we are doing is correct—the *Balance Sheet* (or *(Financial Statement)*) and the *Profit and Loss Statement*, (or *Operating Statement*). Since these two statements are vital to the operation of your business, let us look at them separately and examine the functions of each. Note: all statements from your accountant will carry a "disclaimer" (Figure 12.1).

FIGURE 12.1

XYZ Company, Inc.
1000 Main Street
Dallas, TX 75207

We have reviewed the accompanying balance sheet of XYZ
Company, as of December 31, 19 _ _, and the related statements of income and retained earnings and of changes in
financial position for the year then ended, in accordance with
standard established by the American Institute of Certified
Public Accountants. All information included in these financial statements is the representation of the management of
XYZ Company, Inc.

A review consists principally of inquiries of company personnel
and analytical procedures applied to financial data. It is substantially less in scope than an examination in accordance
with generally accepted auditing standards, the objective of
which is the expression of an opinion regarding the financial
statements taken as a whole. Accordingly, we do not express
such an opinion.

Based on our review, we are not aware of any material modi-
fications that should be made to the accompanying financial
statements in order for them to be in conformity with generally accepted accounting principles.

                                        Certified Public Accountants

Dallas, Texas

January 15, 19 _ _

Balance Sheet, or Financial Statement

This shows you the net worth of your business for a given period of time — ending at a month, a quarter, semiannually, or annually, since these are normal accounting periods. It shows the distribution of the money invested (capital), and it lists your fixed and current assets (what you own) and your current and deferred liabilities (what you owe). By comparing these figures with your own previous experience, or with what is accepted in the trade (since you are a new business), it becomes the guide to proper and efficient management. In short, the balance sheet is a summarized statement of your current financial conditions (Figure 12.2).

Profit and Loss Statement, or Operating Statement

The accepted name for this report within the trade is the *P&L* (Figures 12.3, 12.4, 12.5). As with the *Balance Sheet*, it is prepared for a specific period of time. Usually the two reports are prepared at the same time to cover the same period. The information provided here is net sales, cost of merchandise sold, expenses, and —finally—whether you made a profit or suffered a loss. This statement, when used in tandem with your other reports, shows what expenses must be altered to maintain the budget or be changed to control the expenditures.

I may have been guilty of oversimplification when describing the *Balance Sheet* and P&L, but these are not prepared *by* you, only *for* you. They are prepared by your accountant. He writes them—you read them. What I have tried to do here is give you a thumbnail sketch of what to expect. Turn to your accountant for more detailed explanations.

You have probably heard economists speak of *"ratios."* Another word for ratio is *"comparison."* To break it down to simple terminology, what we are doing is comparing the *P&L* to the *Balance Sheet* during related time periods to arrive at the ratio.

Figure 12.2

XYZ Company, Inc.

Balance Sheet
December 31, 19_ _

Assets

Current assets:		
Cash	$ 550	
Accounts receivable	24,000	
Inventory	25,000	
Total current assets	$49,550	
Property, fixtures, and equipment:		
Leasehold improvements	$ 7,500	
Fixtures	1,500	
Automobiles	6,000	
	$15,000	
Less accumulated depreciation	1,200	13,800
Other assets		650
		$64,000

Liabilities and shareholders' equity

Current liabilities:		
Note payable—current maturity	$14,650	
Accounts payable	17,000	
Accrued expenses	3,000	
Federal income tax payable	350	
Total current liabilities		$35,000
Long-term debt—less current maturity		23,000
Shareholders' equity:		
Common stock	$ 1,000	
Retained earnings	5,000	
Total shareholders' equity		6,000
		$64,000

See accountants' review report.

The notes to financial statements are an integral part of this statement.

FIGURE 12.3

XYZ Company, Inc.
Statement of Income and Retained Earnings
For the Year Ended December 31, 19_ _

Sales—net		$127,000
Cost of goods sold:		
Beginning inventory	$ 20,000	
Purchase	80,000	
Freight	1,350	
	$101,350	
Less ending inventory	25,000	
Cost of goods sold		76,350
Gross profit		$ 50,650
Operating expenses:		
Wages	$ 30,000	
Advertising	7,500	
Auto expense	1,000	
Utilities	500	
Office expense	1,200	
Telephone	750	
Payroll taxes	500	
Other taxes	250	
Insurance	1,400	
Interest	2,000	
Depreciation	700	
Professional fees	2,000	
Repairs and maintenance	800	
Total operating expenses		48,600
Income before income taxes		$ 2,050
Provision for income taxes		350
Net income		$ 1,700
Retained earnings:		
Beginning of year		3,300
End of year		$ 5,000

See accountants' review report.

The notes to financial statements are an integral part of this statement.

FIGURE 12.4

XYZ Company, Inc.
Statement of Changes in Financial Position
for the Year Ended December 31, 19_ _

Funds were provided by:

Net income from operations	$ 1,700	
Noncash charges:		
Depreciation	700	
	$ 2,400	
Increase in long-term debt,		
net of current maturities	3,000	
Total funds provided		$ 5,400

Funds were used for:

Repayment of long-term debt	$ 2,000	
Acquisition of fixtures and equipment	1,500	
Total funds used		3,500

Increase in working capital $ 1,900

Working capital:

Beginning of year	12,650
End of year	$14,550

Increase (decrease) in working capital components:

Cash	300	
Accounts receivable	2,000	
Inventory	(500)	
Notes payable	1,000	
Accounts payable	(1,300)	
Accrued expenses	500	
Federal income tax payable	(100)	
Increase in working capital		$ 1,900

See accountants' review report.
The notes to financial statements are an integral part of this
   statement.[See Fig. 12.5]

FIGURE 12.5

XYZ Company, Inc.

Notes to Financial Statements
December 31, 19_ _

Note A: Summary of significant accounting policies:

Inventory
   The inventory of merchandise is stated as the lower of cost and market—whichever is lower—on a first-in, first-out basis.

Property, fixtures, and equipment
   Property, fixtures, and equipment are stated at cost. Depreciation is calculated by the straight-line method over the estimated useful life of the item.

Income taxes
   The provision for income taxes is based on the current year's income.

   What items, then, relate to one another when determining ratio? *Debt* to *net worth; assets* to *liabilities;* "*turn*" to *capital and net worth;* and *net profits* to *net worth, sales inventory,* and "*turn*" in accounts receivables. By comparing these *ratios* to those accepted as proper (ask your accountant) by businesses of your type and size, you look for problem areas, correct them, and hopefully assure yourself of a profitable operation.
   I have skimmed over record-keeping because I could not possibly cover all the various records you will find yourself keeping once you open your front door. Long before you get started, you will have met with your accountant, and he will show you exactly what records you must maintain so that you can supply him with the proper information to do his

job. What you as a store-owner need to know is *what reports you need* and what these reports *should tell you*—but not particularly *how to prepare them*. You must acquire a basic knowledge, but you're the *boss*—not the *bookkeeper*.

Your Line of Credit

I have tried to tell you what your financial statement (Balance Sheet) should provide you as the owner of a business. Your statement serves still another, and vital, service: it helps establish your line of credit with resources from which you hope to buy. On your first trip to market, you should have several copies of your financial statement with you. When placing an order, give them a copy to facilitate the processing of your order through their credit department. Always remember, most credit managers are people saddled with a job that is not exactly conducive to happiness, so anything you can do to make their lives easier will go a long way toward making your relationship with them more pleasant.

I have seen many *first-time* buyers come to market armed only with a checkbook. This will get you goods but sets the worst possible precedent and does nothing to establish you as a serious buyer and a desirable account to be courted.

I used the term *line of credit*. This is the amount established by each manufacturer to set forth the maximum that you may owe at any given time. Most manufacturers use a credit-checking agency to establish this line; therefore, it is a wise idea also to mail these agencies a copy of your statement before going to market or trying to place orders—that is, of course, if you know which agencies you will need. Since many manufacturers in today's economy use "factors," it is also smart to send them statements, too.

This should be a good place to explain the difference between a *credit-checking agency* and a *factor*.

Credit Agency

Credit agencies are a service that manufacturers employ to recommend which accounts should be extended credit and which should not. Although the manufacturers are not legally bound to adhere to their suggestions, they usually do. If an agency suggests a $1000 line, you will find it difficult to buy more than that amount from any single firm using that agency. This does not mean that you are limited to that amount by all firms combined using that particular agency. *Example:* You are buying from 10 different firms using the ABC credit agency. You can buy $1000 from each for a total of $10,000. Theoretically you could go to market and buy $1,000,000 worth of goods with your $1000 line if you bought from one thousand different firms. It is also a fact of financial life that not every credit agency will set the same limit on you. The limit is a judgment call by the agency's credit manager.

Factor

The factor's main purpose is to supply needed cash flow to a manufacturer by using accounts receivable as the basis for establishing the amount of money to be advanced. The factor buys the manufacturer's receivables outright as they are created by shipping goods. After the factor has approved the credit of the store buying the merchandise, he usually assumes all the risks of collection, and the store now owes the factor, not the resource from whom the goods were purchased.

The following is a step-by-step outline of how a factoring program operates. It can vary slightly between factors, but these five steps generally hold true.:

1. The manufacturer notifies the factor that he has booked an order with your store.
2. The factor then makes all the necessary credit checks and reports back to the manufacturer.

3. The manufacturer ships the order to your store (if your credit has been approved) and sends invoices—one to the store and two copies to the factor. The invoice will carry a notice to the store that your account has been assigned to the factor, and the bill should be paid directly to him.
4. On receipt of the invoices by the factor, he will immediately credit the manufacturer's account for the amount less the factor's finance charge.
5. The manufacturer from that point on can draw out all or any part of the account depending on the terms of the manufacturer's contract with the factor.

Under this arrangement, the manufacturer has received cash on which to operate, the factor has made his percentage, and you have received your merchandise. This is a common practice in the apparel industry today.

Paper Work

In our next chapter, "You and the Government," we will go into some detail concerning the cost of government regulations and the paperwork they create. Here we will note that business managers are often guilty of creating their own paper pyre on which to burn profits. The cost of excessive paperwork is a direct charge to profits. You may think, as a small-business operator, that the control of paperwork (another name for records) is not your problem but rather belongs with the controller of large department stores. This is not true. As a store owner, you will wear many hats: buyer, manager, janitor, salesperson, receiving room clerk, boss, and controller. This last is one of the most important.

What is a controller? One who controls. And *what* does a controller control? Expenses! Since paperwork is a controllable expense—control it!

The secret of proper record retention is to make a mole hill out of a mountain.

Let's call this process *paper retention control*. The unnecessary creation and retention of paper is a constant struggle to control. As it is, you will be inundated with *necessary* paper such as sales slips, invoices, correspondence, personnel files, government information records, bills of lading, credit forms, old ads, new ads, clip services, canceled checks, ledgers, and so on.

Since it is necessary to keep certain records, the creation of additional paperwork increases the chance of errors. Errors are a natural possibility when dealing with the human factor. Therefore, it follows that the less you do, the less chance you have to make mistakes.

Let's assume that you will keep only that paper which is an absolute must. Even this amount must be controlled for maximum efficiency and minimum errors. If these two goals can be reached, you will have achieved certain advantages:

1. You reduce the time you will have to spend reading, sorting, and storing.
2. You save money and space—money that you would have to spend on such items as additional forms, filing cabinets, desks—and the space that each of the items requires.
3. Your people—and, more importantly, you yourself—will be more efficient if you concentrate on the things you must and do not clog your mind with extraneous information.
4. What you do retain will be in a form that can be easily digested.

None of the above comes about without paper retention control. Previously, I have used this expression to mean only the *creation* of paperwork. Equally important is the *longevity* you permit each piece of paper to enjoy.

You have absolutely no control on the amount of paper coming to your business, but you have absolute control on what gets thrown out. Now is the time to mention a vital piece of office equipment—the wastebasket! The person who invented the wastebasket must have been a person in business who received more junk mail than it was possible to keep!

In my business I had a most capable office manager who would shortstop any incoming mail and put only that which required my personal attention on my desk. She was ruthless in disposing immediately of junk mail, answering correspondence, replacing old catalogues when new ones came in, and jotting down notes in the corner of the letters I needed to answer. If you can't afford to hire such a person, you must be just this kind of office manager yourself.

It has been said we live in a plastic world. I feel a more apt description would be *paper* world.

A very simple criterion can be applied to any record you consider maintaining: what future use can it be put to and what later benefit will you received by having it for reference? To answer this ask yourself the following questions:

1. Is the information that I will derive from the record available to me somewhere else (perhaps in a different form)?
2. Do I have to write this same letter so often that a simple form letter would suffice?
3. Do I have two or more records that could be combined to give me essentially the same information?
4. Last, and probably most important, how vital is the information, and how will I use it later?

As a small-store owner you are in a position to see to all of the above and trim your paper consumption. As a small-business person you can do this more easily than the chairman of the board of a large corporation. You should be as familiar as possible with the function of each record that you keep.

Microfilm?

No matter how I tried to eliminate unnecessary records, I found myself building a mountain of paper. It was at this point that I went the microfilm route. You are probably thinking "I am going to operate a *small* store; isn't microfilming for big companies?" The answer is yes, no, and maybe.

In the beginning, there is no need for microfilm. The amount of paper generated will not warrant the expense. But as your business grows and you accumulate years of backlog, you may want to consider microfilm in order to save space and accelerate your administrative operation.

If and when you decide to microfilm your records, you have several choices: (1) you can use a service that will do the actual filming, and you keep a viewer in your office; (2) you can do it yourself with rented equipment; (3) you can buy your own equipment. The size of your business and the amount of capital investment you wish to make will be your deciding factors.

If you consider microfilming as a space-saver only, give it very serious thought. Be sure you consider all the costs this will involve as compared to the money it will cost you simply to store your paper in cardboard boxes on shelves in a back room. For years I do not know how we would have survived in the area of record storage without shoe and shirt boxes. They were invaluable.

To sum up the message of this chapter: your bookkeeping system should provide you with the information you need to help you run your business and tell the government what they want to know in the easiest possible way.

The key words to remember in record-keeping are *simplicity* and *accuracy*. The words to avoid are *curiosity* and *abundance*.

Fourteen

You and The Government

*City, county, state and federal laws. . .
and then there was you!*

You, as a member of the business community, have two basic areas of responsibility: society and the government, each of which has its own set of demands to be met by you, the rookie on the business team. The first, society, includes such social "obligations" as your service to the Scouts, the United Fund, the Salvation Army, Rotary, plus various religious organizations. These "obligations" are really your repayment to the community for the privilege of doing business in its midst. Aside from the obvious PR benefit, service of this kind will make you feel good. The second, the area of government-created responsibility, is the concern of this chapter. Government regulations, which in most cases are necessary, can, and in a great many cases do, stifle business by dint of their sheer number and the high costs of compliance. The seeming maze of Federal rules and regulations is sufficiently complex and variable to enable us to cover it only briefly. We shall try, however, to furnish an adequate overview of how government regulations affect the small-business person.

Although the impact of these regulations is tremendous (and in some instances harmful), no one should be advocating the elimination of all regulations or disagreeing with the ideal of protecting the individual consumer. However, as members of the business community, we cannot fail to be aware of the added cost of these regulations (in paperwork alone), to the total cost of our operations. Business is spending $25 to $35 billion dollars yearly to fill out a mountain of forms. Thus while the cost of governmental administration is huge, the even larger cost is borne by the business sector in complying with these regulations. And while there is no specific set of regulations geared to the apparel industry, still, like all businesses in America, we in the retail field are basically affected by them all. To name just a few: environmental regulations, chemical regulations that affect the manufacturer of synthetic fibers, labeling laws, the cost of regulation fire retardants, the effect on all prices of the minimum wage, protectionism against imports (which do not work anyway)—all add up to big bucks from small business.

As a small-business person, you face an army of initials: CSHA, ERISA, USDA, SEC, EEOC, FDA EIA, DOD, DOT, FTC, IRS; and these are just some of the ones from Washington. Let us not forget state and local agencies.

In some cases we see one agency's authority overlapping that of another. It is not unusual that in being in compliance with one set of rules, you can be in violation of another. If we reach the point where overregulation stifles creativity, we are in trouble, since creativity is the hallmark of our industry.

So as not to leave you with the impression that the federal government is completely oblivious of this situation, Congress passed the Regulatory Flexibility Act of 1980 which was signed into law by President Jimmy Carter. This act provides for public notices to be posted before any new regulations can be installed, thus giving small business an opportunity to participate in the drafting of these regulations. Finally, all Federal agencies are required to review existing rules in hopes of reducing their impact on small business.

The new law, which amends the Administrative Procedure Act, became effective January 1, 1981. We must wait and see if the spirit of this act and its implications and implementation will meet and serve the needs of small business. The business community is confident that this spirit of deregulation will be carried forward and even accelerate in the future. Officials and candidates in both major parties are singing this same tune. Many feel that there should be a shift in power from the federal level back to the states, which would tend to decrease the number of regulations imposed on the business community. The deregulation movement is one which all small business people support.

Taxes

Probably the most difficult part of our involvement with the government (after regulation) is in the area of taxes. These come in many forms and disguises, but never let them sneak up on you. Remember, business pays the taxes, and you as a businessperson either pay the tax directly or create the jobs and sales that in turn pay the taxes! Since taxes support all levels of government, government therefore should be responsive to the needs of business. Time is money when *you* become a tax collector (payroll and sales), a safety inspector (OSHA), a civil rights protector (EEOC) and many other things; it becomes a business cost of which you should be aware. Uncle Sam is coming to town.

Tax rules and regulations vary from city to city and state to state. Only federal-taxes are uniform throughout the nation. All states today have a state sales tax, as do most cities; this will be from 4 percent upward for the state, with the city sales tax added to that. In addition to these there are personal property taxes, school taxes, county taxes, and so on. You may even be living in a state that also has both personal income taxes and state corporative income taxes. Florida, Nevada, South Dakota, Texas, Washington, and Wyoming have no per capita individual income tax. Nevada, Texas, Washington, and Wyoming have no corporate income tax as a percentage of total state tax revenue.

The prime responsibility for the collection of all of these taxes rests completely with you as the owner of a business. Payroll deduction and Social Security taxes are withheld from employees' pay and remitted to the proper authority. State sales taxes are remitted to the state. You must keep proper records (remember Chapter 13) to substantiate all payments.

In the realm of state government, the agency with which you will most often come in contact is the State Comptroller's Office. In your state it may be known by a different name, but it always spells "tax collector." As we said earlier, you must collect state sales tax and pay it to the proper state office.

Finally, where will you find out how many and what kind of rules and regulations you must adhere to? As with many other matters discussed so far, consultation with your attorney and accountant is a must.

Ordinances: Safety and Zoning

Every business must have a license to operate. Since licensing laws vary not only from state to state but from city to city, it would be impossible to list all of the requirements in this book. It suffices to say that you should check with your attorney and make sure that your house is legally in order before you open your front door.

In addition to the license required to run a business, there are the many city ordinances that govern the construction of the building. These ordinances are a many-splendored array

not a four-letter word. It is not only the responsibility of lob-byists to contact legislators on behalf of those they represent —they must report back to their clients and keep them informed.

The following, by Congressman Henry Hyde (Rep., Ill.) beautifully sums up Congress's view of citizens' rights and their obligation to act in their own behalf; he agrees with House Speaker Tip O'Neill that "Everybody has a lobby," but says that there are lobbies and there are lobbies: some are not nearly as effective as other.

Businessmen too often ignore important legislation until it reaches the House or Senate floor and then they may send their congressman a brusque mailgram demanding that he vote the right way. This is better than noth-ing, but often it is too little and much too late. Any bill that reaches the floor has gone through subcommittee and full committee, through hearings and markup. Businessmen objecting to a bill, or portions of a bill, should make their views known as early and as often as common sense dictates.

Anyone who can relate the essential aspects of a bill to the people in a congressman's own district—how it may affect industry, unemployment, wages, etc.—is performing a valuable service for that congressman as well as himself.

Their personal touch is almost important. A number of businesses initi-ate correspondence by passing out preprinted postcards for their employees to sign and mail, but it's not as effective as personal contact.

Don't take a congressman for granted because he may or may not have been in your corner in the past.

Cultivate a good working relationship with both the congressman and his staff, particularly the legislative assistant, who will keep the congress-man informed of constituents' visits, phone calls, and concerns.

Prepare concise, well-researched position papers. These are much more effective than a phone call to a busy congressional office. If you plan to visit the office, bring the position paper with you; if not, mail it.

If I may, let me relate a personal observation. I have been privileged to visit with and watch our elected officials in action both in the halls of Congress and my state capital.

Like most of the citizenry watching the 6 o'clock news or reading the daily papers, my thinking and opinions were shaped by men and women looking into the government than by speaking to those on the inside looking out.

The game is the same, only the viewpoint is different.

In this post-Watergate age, we are apt to be led down the path of distrust and skepticism with regard to the actions and behavior of those men and women whom we have elected to serve us as our representatives.

In conversations with various members of Congress, I never lost sight of the questions that affect us both as businesspeople and as citizens. It is vital that our legislators be kept constantly aware of the issues facing the business community. Washington is closer than the time it takes a plane to fly there. It is instantaneous, and the effect is one of lasting importance.

We may sometimes feel that it is naive to let our positions be known, but we must never be lulled into thinking that our elected officials do not listen or do not care. *This is not true*; they *do* listen, and they *do* act. The way they act depends on who presents his side of an issue in the most convincing and creditable fashion.

It is easy to condemn; it is easy to correct; but it is *not* easy to understand and appreciate the pressures under which the members of Congress and our state houses must operate.

If I have learned one thing from my various trips to the seats of government, it is that these men and women are for the most part hard-working and dedicated public servants. This is not to imply in any way that they are perfect and never make mistakes. It is merely to remind us that for all their imperfections, they are doing a good job, under what are often the most stringent conditions.

If we as citizens give our support and voice our opinion, we will receive our *just due*. There is no free ride in business or in life. We get what we earn.

Fifteen

The Last Word

*In the end there was no sun,
the world was engulfed in darkness
and nothing on the earth moved...
except a shopper looking for an open store
and a merchant looking for that last customer*

An author can be pardoned, after pages and pages of his own writing, if he wants to have the last word. Actually, it is you who will really have the last word as evidenced by just what you do with all you have learned and tried to master—what advice you will accept, what you will bypass in favor of having it your way or just playing your hunch or intuition. Of course, all that depends on whether you are still interested in being a merchant.

If by this time you are not convinced that opening a store is sheer madness and that playing golf or bridge and letting someone else support you is your inalienable right—then this book has been at least partially successful.

It has been said, "You don't have to be crazy to be a merchant...but it helps." We'll assume that this was meant in jest! So if you haven't been talked out of what sometimes

211

seems a madcap way to make a dollar—then welcome to that great fraternity (or sorority, if you wish) of others who have taken the step of opening their own store before you. Despite the occasional heartache and grey hairs, it is a very rewarding and even noble endeavor.

As I said in the opening paragraph of this book: "In my 25 years as a store manager, buyer, merchandise manager, and finally as the president and owner/partner of 14 ladies' and men's apparel specialty stores, I learned many things—but above all, I learned that owning and managing your own retail store is a grueling challenge and one of the most rewarding experiences in life." The opportunity awaiting you (to say nothing of the challenge) is one of daring, excitement, love, and emotions not yet experienced.

Why Small is Beautiful

Over the past 30 years, the number of small businesses in the United States has grown steadily. It is almost one of nature's unexplained miracles that small businesses withstand economic downturns better than their big brothers and sisters.

There is no single foolproof answer to why it is sometimes better to be small than large. There is, however, some good country logic as to why it might be so.

Small-store operators are "on-the-premises-supervisor-owner-managers." The key words here are *on-the-premises* and *supervisor*. The mere fact that you are in your store every day watching details is a tremendous advantage over absentee management, who must rely on someone else. You can turn on a dime when you see something happening that requires corrective action.

If you have paid attention to what was said in the chapter on Records and Bookkeeping, you should know that small businesses do not have complicated systems that encumber action and cost you all of your profits to maintain.

Small businesses afford the owner the opportunity to occasionally stop and smell the flowers beside the road. This may not seem a reason for success, but talk to any harried executive of a large corporation, and you may well see a glint of envy in his eye. A rested merchant can think with a clearer mind. This matter of being the sole seat of power with total responsibility and at the same time smelling the flowers may seem paradoxical, but in reality it makes sense.

As a small-business person, your life will not be free of financial worries. You will, more often than not, be concerned over money and up-and-down sales, but a national downturn in the economy will not come as any reason for panic. Alarm, yes; panic, no! The instinct for survival is inherent in the small-businessperson. Therefore, when you join the club, you will have this inborn feeling that nothing is fatal. While the above is said in a spirit of confidence, it should not lull you into a sense of false security.

Throughout this book I have tried to blaze a trail through the forest of doubt that confronts everyone who has considered *shopkeeping* as a vocation. Because of the multitude of things that an aspiring merchant must know, I could not cover every step you will take on your road to success and security in the business community. No book ever written, nor a library of such books, can answer every question, warn you of every pitfall you may encounter, or alert you to every problem you will face.

But I hope that what I have written will in some way light your path to a new and exciting career—that some day you will look back on a successful life as a merchant and feel that the years spent in your store were fruitful and that you enjoyed every minute of your life as a merchant. Well, maybe not *every* minute—but it should be close.

I hope that this book has at least made you aware of some of the things you can expect along the way. Remember, just when you think you know all of the answers, they will change the questions.

I would like to leave you with two thoughts that perhaps sum up what I have been trying to say. The first is mine, the second is Mark Twain's.

1. "The beginning of knowledge is to realize just how little we know."
2. "It ain't what people know that gets them in trouble—it's what they know that ain't so."

If at this point you realize how little you know, and if you now know that some of what you thought you knew *"ain't so"* —then you're ahead of the game.

CASH STAND: That area in the store (counter or office) where sales are written up and/or cash is received.

CHAIN: A group of stores operated by one organization. Usually refers to Sears, Penney, Montgomery Ward, K-Mart, etc.

CHARGE: Permitting a customer to take merchandise out of the store with a promise to pay later.

CHEAPEST AND BEST: Used as a shipping instruction when not designating a specific carrier. It means that the vendor's shipping department must determine the best way to ship you at the cheapest rate possible.

CHECKING: A style that is selling at the retail level. Also means that a credit agency is approving your account for credit.

CHECK-OUT: A record of goods received and sold. Also refers to an individual style that sold quickly.

CLEARANCE: Selling merchandise at a reduced price. Usually refers to a sale pertaining to more than one department.

CLOAKY: An outmoded name for a ladies' coat-and-suit manufacturer.

COLLECTION(S): Monies received on open charge accounts. A line of merchandise produced by a single maker. Usually refers to higher priced goods

CONSIGNMENT: Merchandise purchased from vendor with guarantee of selling or right to return in a specific time. Same as memo or round-trip.

CONTENT LABEL: A tag placed on merchandise setting forth materials used in its production. Required by Federal Law.

CO-OP: Abbreviation for cooperation. Most often applied to advertising arrangements whereby the manufacturer pays part of the cost of an ad featuring the manufacturer's product line.

COST: The price you pay for supplies, services, and merchandise. When used for merchandise, refers only to wholesale price.

CPSC: Consumer Product Safety Commission.

CREDIT: The practice of selling now with a promise of payment later by a prescribed schedule.

CREDIT AGENCY: Organizations that determine and establish lines of credit based on financial information.

CUT 'N SEWN: Describes the manufacturing process of cutting the cloth and sewing it together. Used to differentiate from knitting.

D

DAMAGE: Any irregularity in the merchandise. More severe than a 'flaw.'

DATING: Extra time permitted by the vendor to pay invoices over and above normal terms.

DELIVERY DATE: An agreed-upon time in which a manufacturer must ship your order or it may be canceled at your discretion.

DEPARTMENT: The term used to designate various major categories of merchandise. Also refers to a specific area of the store that contains similar goods.

DISCOUNT: Amount subtracted from retail to create special amount deducted from invoice by vendor as normal reduction for paying bill as per terms.

DOL: Department of Labor.

DOT: Department of Transportation.

E

E.E.O.C.: Equal Employment Opportunity Commission. A federal agency that ensures against discrimination based on race, color, or creed.

EOM: End of month. Used in conjunction with 8/10, which means an 8 percent discount if paid within 10 days after the end of the month.

EPA: Environmental Protection Agency.

ERISA: Employee Retirement Income Security Act.

EXTRA 30: Additional 30 days allowed by the manufacturer to pay over and above normal 8/10 terms.

F

FACTOR: A bank or other financial institution that buys your invoice from the vendor.

FDA: Food and Drug Administration.

FEDS: The Federal government or anyone who works for a federal agency.

FIRST-FLOOR GOODS: Used to describe moderate-priced goods since this is where major stores locate these departments.

FLAW: Denotes a small damage in the merchandise.

FOOTAGE: Size of store given in square feet.

FRONT: Show (display) windows.

FTC: Federal Trade Commission.

G

GONDOLAS: Tiered floor units used to sell from and also to display merchandise.

GOODS: Another name for merchandise.

H

HANDLE: The feel of the cloth when touched.

HANG ROD: The steel rods used in bins or floor racks on which to hang merchandise.

HEAVY HITTERS: Term applied to big buyers or big stores.

HOUSE BOOK: Salesbook kept for noncommission sales. To be differentiated from the salesperson's book.

I

IMPORTS: Any product not made in, but sold in, the United States.

INITIAL MARKUP: The original percentage added to the cost to arrrive at the retail selling price.

INVENTORY: The total amount of merchandise in the store in both units and dollars.

IR'S: Irregulars. Merchandise with flaws.

IRS: Internal Revenue Service.

K

KEYSTONE MARKUP: Refers to the percentage markup applied to the goods. Fifty percent or double the cost.

L

LABEL: A tag sewn into the garment containing any of the following: vendor's name, store name, care intructions, fabric content, and country of origin.

LAYAWAY: Merchandise held out of stock and reserved for a specific customer with deposit. Customer does not receive the goods until paid for completely or the balance is transfered to a charge account.

LINAGE: The total number of lines used in a newspaper ad or ads for a given period.

LINE: A group of samples representing one manufacturer. Usually carried by the salesrep. A division of a newspaper page by which advertising is figured. The amount of credit for which your account has been approved.

LOGO: Distinctive style of lettering for your store name. Same as a "Sig-cut."

LOW END: Refers to cheaper goods. The lowest-priced goods in the line.

LOX: A bad style.

LY: Last year.

M

MAIL-ORDER: Merchandise ordered through the mail. Also applied to that type of ad which includes coupon for buying goods in this manner.

MAINTAINED MARKUP: The percentage over and above the cost of the goods after allowing for expenses (e.g., operations, markdowns).

MAJOR: Refers to large department stores and chains (e.g., Sears, Penney, Allied and Federated Stores).

MAKER: Another name for a manufacturer or vendor.

MALL: A shopping center usually composed of major store(s) and many smaller shops with common covered area.

MAMA-PAPA STORE: Term used to describe a very small store usually run by two or three people.

MARKDOWNS: The percentage or dollars a garment is reduced from its original retail price.

MARKDOWN MONEY: Special allowance given by vendor to help offset losses incurred by markdowns on a bad style.

MARKET: A group of manufacturers showing their lines in the same place at the same time.

MARKUP: The amount (percentage or dollars) added to the wholesale cost to arrive at the retail selling price.

MEMO: Merchandise purchased from vendor with guarantee of selling or right to return. Same as consignment or round trip.

MODERATE: Middle-of-the-road-priced merchandise. Usually found in specialty stores and on the first and second floors of majors.

N

NET: Selling price after deducting discount. Usually refers to wholesale cost.

NUMBER(S): A specific style(s). Short for a "style number."

O

OFF PRICE: (OP'S): Merchandise purchased from vendor at less than original wholesale cost.

ON APPROVAL: Merchandise taken out of the store by a customer with the understanding that it can be returned for credit or refund within an agreed-upon time.

OPEN-TO-BUY (OTB): A trade term used to describe the number of dollars to be spent or units to be bought for any given period of time in each department.

ORDERS: The written purchase agreement between seller and buyer. Same as *paper*.

OSHA: Occupational Safety and Health Administration. Federal agency governing employee working conditions.

P

P & L: Abbreviations for Profit and Loss. Refers to both a type of financial statement and a noncollectable charge account.

PAPER: The written purchase agreement between seller and buyer.

PIECES: Individual units of merchandise.

PLASTIC: Slang expression used for describing charge cards issued by banks or individual stores.

POLY: Abbreviation of *polyester*. A synthetic fiber.

PRICE LINES: A range of prices at either wholesale or retail in which you are buying and selling.

PRIVATE LINES: Putting your store's name or any name you have registered on goods bought from an unbranded maker.

PROFIT: The amount remaining after subtracting wholesale cost and all operating costs from total retail.

PROMOTION: Any sale or clearance where price is the factor. Also used to describe off-price goods offered by a manufacturer.

PULL: Garment returned to stock from layaway.

RACKS: Floor stands with hang rod for displaying merchandise. Sometimes used *incorrectly* to describe hangers.

REORDER: The purchasing of additional units of the same style based on quick sales.

REGULAR PRICE: Applied to normal cost or retail selling price.

REP: Abbreviation of *representative*. Refers to a wholesale salesperson.

RETAIL: Selling price to consumer after adding mark-up to cost.

RETURN: Merchandising sent back to manufacturer by a store or by consumer to a store.

ROUNDTRIP: Merchandise purchased from vendor with guarantee of selling or right to return. Same as consignment or memo.

ROUNDER: Circular floor rack used to display merchandise.

RUN OF SIZES: Ordering a single piece of each size of a particular style.

S

SALE: Offering merchandise at a reduced price or referring to the selling of any item.

SALE RINGER: Small string-tag indicating sale price. Usually attached to regular garment ticket.

SBA: Small Business Administration. A Federal agency that assists with business loans and other problems.

SCHMALTZ: The cream of the crop.

SLC: Securities and Exchange Commission.

SHOP: A small store. Also the viewing of many different lines before making final purchases. Used also to describe comparative shopping of competitor.

SHOW: Used primarily to designate a wholesale market.

SHOWCASE: Glass case used to display small items such as jewelry or lingerie.

SHRINKAGE: Merchandise stolen or otherwise missing from inventory.

SIG CUT: The distinctive lettering of your store's name. Same as *logo*.

SOC: An abbreviation used to describe the Society Section of the newspaper.

SPIFF: A bonus paid to a salesperson for selling a specific piece of merchandise. Usually paid over and above normal commission.

SPOT: Advertisement on TV or radio. A soiled area on a garment.

STOCK: Your entire inventory of merchandise.

STYLE NUMBER: Number assigned by a manufacturer to a particular garment as identification.

SWATCH: Sample piece of cloth to show color and fabric.

T

TAKING NUMBERS: Reviewing a manufacturer's line and recording the style numbers you prefer. No order is left at this time.

TRAFFIC: The number of people passing by or shopping in your store.

TRANSPORTATION: The means used to move merchandise from manufacturer to store.

T-STAND: A single-trunk floor rack with either a single or double crossbar. Used for highlighting a limited amount of goods.

TURN: The length of time required to sell the merchandise in a given department or an entire stock. Also applied to collection time for accounts receivable.

U

UNITS: Individual pieces that compose an inventory or an order. Used by chain stores to refer to number of stores.

UPSTAIRS: Used to describe better goods since this is where majors locate their more expensive departments.

USDA: United States Department of Agriculture.

Y

VENDOR: Another name for manufacturer or maker.

W

WHOLESALE: Vendor's price to the retailer. Same as cost.

Z

ZONING: Municipal regulations governing type of business or type of structure permitted in specific areas of a city.

Index